WHAT WE'RE WORTH

WHAT WE'RE WORTH

Realize Your HLV
(Human Life Value)...
And Know What
You're Really Worth!

MICHAEL
G. ISOM

ASSET MIRROR, LLC | SAINT GEORGE, UT

Although the author has made every effort to ensure that the information in this book was correct at press time, the author does not assume and hereby disclaims any liability to any party for any loss, damage, or disruption caused by errors or omissions, whether such errors or omissions result from negligence, accident, or any other cause. This book is also not intended to provide specific financial or legal advice. The author does not assume and hereby disclaims any liability to any party for any loss, damage, or disruption caused by the information in this book. For advice and guidance specific to your situation please contact Vault AIS, or a qualified expert.

Published by
Asset Mirror, LLC | Saint George, UT

Publisher's Cataloging-in-Publication Data

Isom, Michael G.

What we're worth : realize your HLV (human life value) ... and know what you're really worth! / Michael G. Isom. – Saint George, UT : Asset Mirror, LLC, 2023.

p. ; cm.

ISBN13: 978-0-9601191-0-3

1. Life--Fiction. 2. Value--Fiction. I. Title.

PS3609.S66 W43 2023

813.6--dc23

Project coordination by Jenkins Group, Inc. | www.jenkinsgroupinc.com

Interior design by Brooke Camfield

Printed in the United States of America

27 26 25 24 23 • 5 4 3 2 1

DEDICATION

This book is dedicated to the people who made it possible for me to write it:

To my friend and colleague, Garrett Gunderson. Thank you for your example.

To Garrett J. White, your influence in my life has been life-changing.

To my former business partners, the late Ray Hooper and Les McGuire. RIP, Ray and Les. I love and miss you both.

To my assistant, Lacey Yurkew, who has been part of my growth journey and watched me rise and fall and rise again over the years. My, how we've grown together.

Finally, to my family:

My wife, Wendy. Thank you for believing in me when I did not. Our love, trust, and friendship are second to none. We are soulmates.

Our son, Kadin. You inspire me daily.

Our daughter, Kennedy; her fiancé, Corbin; and their son, Weston—our grandson. The foundation you are building is priceless.

We are the Wolf Pack. We run together, and we love and trust one another. We may go away for a while, but we'll always come back together and be there for one another.

CONTENTS

CHAPTER 1

SUDDENLY, THEN ALL AT ONCE

The first rule of investing is, don't lose [money].
And the second rule of investing is, don't forget the first rule.
And that's all the rules there are.

—Warren Buffett

"No. No, no, no. Oh, nonononono *no*, this can't be happening. NO!"

Seated at the simple wooden desk in his home office, staring almost vacantly at his computer monitor, David Shallcross felt a burst of nausea like a liquid firecracker at the back of his throat. Everything he'd achieved in his entire life had just vanished, slipping from his grasp like a tightly clutched fistful of mercury.

He was reading *The New York Times* online, and the article that bore the bad news had been published a full eight hours earlier. David lived in Southern California, three hours behind New York time, and having decided to take the day off, he'd slept in a bit. It was now already 1:00 p.m. in New York, far too late for him to do anything about the situation. He was ruined.

He'd taken the day off because . . . well, why *not* take a day off at this point? As of the previous week, he was effectively retired at the age of forty-six—or so he'd thought. SafeTech, the cybersecurity consulting firm he'd painstakingly built over the last twenty years, was floundering since his former partner had split on him, gutting their shared business in the process. *To hell with him*, David had decided, *and to hell with this business*. He'd paid each of his remaining employees a generous severance package, then just shut the whole operation down. David didn't want to be a cybersecurity consultant anymore, and he no longer *needed* to be one. Or so he'd thought. During the past six months, he'd made a killing in cryptocurrency, investing in a new digital coin called Ephemerum.

The venture had begun with a cautious, toe-in-the-water investment of $100,000—chump change for a man of David's means—that had nearly tripled in value within a month. A breathless piece in *Fortune* magazine had proclaimed Ephemerum (commonly known in the tech and banking worlds as "Eph") to be "a Bitcoin killer" that would set a new industry standard of security and value, and David had seen no red flags that might have contradicted that assessment. Sure, there had been one or two Debbie Downers at *The Economist* and *National Review* who'd warned that Ephemerum was a speculation bubble waiting to burst, but David had found their arguments unpersuasive—timid, even. He had a healthy respect for his own judgment and courage, and he had believed unreservedly that his reward for investing in Eph would be an endless rain of money falling on him for the remainder of his life.

And now I'm royally Eph'd, he thought bitterly.

He wondered how he had he gotten to this point. But there was no use in pretending he didn't know exactly how it had happened: he had been reckless. He had invested more than he could afford to lose—i.e., *everything*. He had wagered his future, and his family's future, on what had turned out to be a bad bet.

His family! Oh, dear God, how would they take it when they found out? The face of his wife, Sandy, suddenly filled his mind, momentarily crowding out all other thoughts. What would she say? Her rage—her *justified* fury, against which no defense was possible—was too terrible even to imagine. And how would his children react to the realization that their father had ultimately failed to provide even for their most basic needs? David Jr. idolized his father—of course he did, he was nine—and would doubtless love his dad no matter what. That realization pierced David's shock and brought tears of gratitude and shame to his eyes. He knew he didn't even remotely deserve that kind of unequivocal love. Still, it was comforting to have it, even if, when DJ got older and acquired an adult understanding of his reduced circumstances, he was bound to judge his old man a bit more harshly. He imagined his adult son saying to a psychologist, "My dad probably did the best he could for us, but he was weak and careless—and that's why I turned out a failure, just like him."

As for the girls, Amy and Chelsea: they were in high school, at the exact age when a child's relationship with her parents is maximally fraught. They might never forgive him. *The best I can probably hope for,* he thought, *is that they don't develop "daddy issues" and end up getting involved with an endless series of predatory men.*

The rational part of his mind reasserted itself for a moment and threw a bucket of cold water on his self-pity. *Stop it,* he told himself. *For God's sake, focus your attention on what matters* now. *What can you do about this? How did you even get here?*

That thought kept coming back, like a song that gets stuck in your head and won't go away. He realized he had overestimated his own expertise—exhibiting exactly the kind of failure of imagination that he despised when he saw it in others.

Ephemerum, it turned out, had multiple vulnerabilities—which he should have been able to spot. For crying out loud, that was what he *did* for a living! True, other cybersecurity experts—people just like him employed by Ephemerum and the various cryptocurrency exchanges that dealt in it—must have also failed to raise the alarm. But that was cold comfort. Some Belarusian hackers *had* spotted those vulnerabilities, and their perceptiveness had netted them $20 million worth of stolen Ephcoins. And he should have realized that such a heist was possible.

In and of itself, the $20 million loss wasn't the end of the world; as a company, Ephemerum was worth a heck of a lot more than that. No, the nuclear bomb that would destroy the company and its currency was the sudden collapse of the public's faith in it. In the hours after that story in *The Times* had been published—while David slept contentedly in his Hästens bed, blissfully oblivious—twenty-two million people had jumped out of Ephemerum as frantically as those kids had jumped out of the pool in that infamous scene from *Caddyshack.* By the time David was up and making his coffee, the price of one Ephcoin had dropped from $4,270 to $4, and his investment was now worthless.

Running his fingers through his immaculately styled blond hair, David took inventory of what he'd put on the line. The staggering stupidity of what he had done suddenly swelled in his mind like a balloon. When his $100K investment had blown up into a quarter-million dollars in a matter of weeks, he had become drunk on his success—drunk and greedy. Gradually at first, and then suddenly, he'd pushed all his chips to the center of the table, making ever-larger investments that generated ever-larger returns.

And then at some point, without even realizing it, he'd stepped off the ledge of rationality: first he'd liquidated all his other investments and plowed them into Ephemerum. Then he'd invested all of his personal savings.

He'd drained his retirement accounts, then the brokerage accounts he shared with Sandy, throwing in the contents of their joint checking account, leaving only enough for a couple months' expenses. He'd invested everything but the change in DJ's piggy bank, which sat innocently in his upstairs bedroom next to his Little League trophies, inanimate and therefore unaware of its own narrow escape from the hammer.

And finally, unforgivably, he'd even wormed his way into Sandy's 401(k), and taken that, too. He'd actually thought, as he committed this betrayal, that he was doing her a favor—that he could put double the amount he'd quietly lifted back into the account, and she'd be surprised and delighted when she discovered the gift.

As the true reprehensibility of this act finally sunk in, David's growing nausea suddenly overtook him. Unable to get up and run to the bathroom in time, he puked into his office wastebasket.

Then he fainted.

When he came to, he glanced at his watch to see how long he'd been lying there. It was 10:30 a.m. He'd been out only for a couple minutes, but Sandy, who had left the house to take the kids to school and meet a friend for breakfast while he was sleeping, would be back soon. And then he would have to tell her what had happened—what he'd done. There was no putting it off: with the kids at school, no better time would present itself. Besides, he was too badly shaken to lie convincingly.

As that thought came to him, David heard Sandy's car in the driveway. He took a deep breath, trying to banish the sick feeling that seemed to emanate simultaneously from his heart and his stomach. He didn't know how the conversation was going to start . . . but he knew it wasn't going to end well.

The story of David and Sandy's courtship was so wholesome it would have been corny if it weren't true. They'd met during high school, while they were both working at the In-N-Out Burger next to the Laguna Inn hotel on Camino Capistrano, right by the 5 freeway. The moment he'd first laid eyes on Sandy Harper, David had been instantly smitten—another corny aspect of the story, but easy to believe when David told it, because she was beautiful. Not just pretty, but movie-star beautiful, with long, dark brown hair (David had a weakness for brunettes), bewitching green eyes, and the kind of figure that caused traffic accidents.

And yet, she'd been shy. This was not the affected shyness of a pretty, popular girl who knows that all the boys get sweaty and panicky when she walks by, but rather a genuine shyness that was probably an outgrowth of her bookish nature. As for popularity . . . Sandy's beauty ensured that she was well-liked, but her shyness and her distaste for cheap compliments limited how high her social standing could rise. Despite her beauty, Sandy wasn't the prom queen, and was never going to be.

David, on the other hand, *was* popular—the proverbial golden boy, the star pitcher on his school's baseball team, and somehow an honor student besides. In fact, if he and Sandy had gone to the same high school, her knowledge of his status would have foreclosed any possibility of a relationship between them. The easy, confident, in-group laughter of socially better-situated kids grated on her ears, as it grates on the ears of most introverted, socially awkward kids, and she probably wouldn't have given David the time of day.

But she didn't know, and long before she found out, his natural charm had won her over. He was as confident as she was diffident . . . and he was *funny*. At work, he'd do weird things like putting plastic googly-eyes on hamburger buns and making them talk to each other like hand puppets. Whenever he and Sandy worked a shift together, David's unselfconscious silliness caused the hours to pass too quickly, despite the menial nature of their jobs. And when the shift ended, she'd find herself checking the schedule on her way out the door to see if they would be working together the next day.

Unbeknownst to Sandy, David did the same thing—and eventually he started coming into the restaurant on days when she was working and he wasn't, on the pretext of grabbing a quick meal. Sometimes he'd drop by because he "happened to be in the neighborhood," although he never said what for.

On one of these occasions, he finally asked her out—so clumsily and awkwardly that at first Sandy thought he was just being silly in his usual way. She was on her break, standing out in the parking lot getting a little sun. At the sight of his green Honda Civic pulling into the lot, her heart suddenly doubled its tempo—as it always did when she saw him, even after many years of marriage.

Exiting the car, David appeared to take sudden notice of Sandy, and what appeared to be a smile of spontaneous delight bloomed on his face as he approached her. It would be years before it occurred to her that this "Oh, fancy running into you here" expression was a well-rehearsed performance. Of course he knew perfectly well that she was working that day, and had a good idea what time she'd probably go on her break.

"Hey, stranger!" she said with faux coolness. She quickly fished a Tic Tac out of her purse.

"Hey good-lookin', what's cookin'?" David said in his impeccable Bart Simpson-impression voice. The "what's cooking" joke was lame on its own merit, because of where they worked, and delivering the line in that voice made no sense at all . . . but he knew the Bart voice always made Sandy laugh, and nothing—not baseball, not his car, not the sun itself—meant as much to David as making Sandy laugh.

"Burgers, you nimrod, what do you think?" she replied. "We don't make sushi here."

"*Ay, caramba,*" David said, hanging his head in mock misery. Sandy giggled like the seventeen-year-old schoolgirl she was, and David went nearly stone-faced in an effort to mask his joy.

"So what brings you 'round here today?" she asked, as nonchalantly as she could.

"Oh, not much . . . just, umm, stopping by for a cup of coffee while I'm in the area." David's normally deep and confident voice cracked on every third vowel, and for a moment Sandy thought he was doing another *Simpsons* impression, of the pimply teenager who worked at Krusty Burger—which would have been apt. But then he cleared his throat and coughed, and she realized the tremor in his voice had been genuine. *What's the matter with him?* she thought.

"Hey, uhh, what are you doing Friday night?" he suddenly said, with carefully feigned and utterly unconvincing casualness, as though it had only just now, out of the blue, occurred to him to ask, maybe because an opening had suddenly appeared in his busy social calendar.

Twenty-seven-year-old Sandy Shallcross would one day laugh at this memory of her nervous, lovestruck husband, but seventeen-year-old Sandy Harper was too shocked and overjoyed to notice how funny he was being (unintentionally, for once). In her mind's eye, she leapt into his arms and he carried her away somewhere, to a place far, far away from In-N-Out Burger.

"Hmm," she said. "Y'know, I actually don't think I have any plans." As though she wouldn't have cancelled life-saving heart surgery to go out with him that weekend.

From that day forward, David and Sandy never spent another weekend apart. Recalling that moment now, as he heard her heels click-clacking on the front walk, her keys jingling as she dropped them back into her purse. David thought that if he had a time machine, he would go back to the day he bought his first Ephcoin and murder his younger self. He'd rather see himself dead than have to tell Sandy what he was about to tell her.

"Oh, you're finally up!" she said, as she swung open the door. She walked into the kitchen and over to the chair where David sat, brooding, his face as vacant as a dead man's. She kissed the top of his head. "Save me any coffee?"

David sighed deeply, the pounding of his heart belied by his slack-jawed expression. "No," he said, "I didn't. I guess that makes me kind of a jerk. Yeah, that's what I am—" his voice began to crack, just as it had on the day he'd first asked her out, "a selfish *jerk*." With that, his voice broke entirely, and he could no longer make any other sound but a series of ugly, hitching, blubbery sobs.

"Oh, honey, no! What is it?" Sandy said, putting her arms around him. David didn't get up from the chair. He just sat, his head wrapped in his arms and pressed into the table, guttural, incoherent toddler-howls emanating from the deepest parts of his anatomy.

When, after a few minutes, he had regained some semblance of composure, he lifted his head and began, slowly and haltingly, to speak. He started by telling her what he'd read in *The Times*. She knew he'd invested a good-sized chunk of cash in Ephemerum, but that didn't begin to explain the inconsolable puddle of a man sitting before her.

"Okay, so how much did you lose?" she asked.

"Everything," he said.

"Well, yeah, obviously your entire investment is gone. But it's only money, baby. We'll make more. *You'll* make more."

"No," he said, still out of breath from his crying jag. "You don't get it. I mean *everything*."

For a split-second, total understanding flashed into her mind . . . but then it was gone. That couldn't possibly be what he meant. "What do you mean 'everything?'" she asked.

"Just what I said. Everything. All of it. *Everything*. My personal savings. All my other investments—"

"Oh, honey—"

"Most of what was in our joint checking account . . ."

She felt ashamed of the momentary flash of anger she now felt; why kick the man when he's down? "Geez, baby—"

"Our retirement accounts—"

"WHAT?" He couldn't be serious. Was this some weird, ill-conceived prank?

"And your 401(k)." His voice was now barely above a whisper.

She stared at him, silently, for a long time, her mouth half open, her face as blank as his own. "How . . . how the hell did you even do that? I . . . I had $380,000 in there! How did you get my . . . never mind, I guess it's . . . dammit, David, why?"

His face was red and streaked with tears, and his jaw bobbed senselessly up and down, but no sound came out. He suddenly looked like a little child, and it seemed to her that her question hadn't even registered.

"Sweetheart, I'm so sorry," he finally said. It was such a grotesquely inadequate response . . . but what else was there to say?

"I SAID, *WHY!*" she shouted. She hated the confusion of feelings flooding her psyche:

she wanted to slap him, right in that stupid, mewling, blubbery face of his. But he was her husband and she loved him—every bit as much now as the day she'd met him—and wanted to comfort and console him . . . and gouge his eyes out. She wanted to take his sad, miserable face lovingly in her hands and grab him by the ears and comfort his face with her knee.

He was talking again, she realized, probably trying to answer her *why* question. Since she hadn't been listening anyway, she interrupted him. "What do we have left?"

David sighed again and stared at his shoes. "The house, I guess, although we have no way to make payments now that my business is gone."

"Can't you revive it? I know you were planning a luxurious early retirement, but–"

"No, Ben took everything when he left. Half of our people went with him to his new venture, and he took two-thirds of our billables with him. What's left isn't enough to sustain operations. I can't rebuild from that–certainly not from the state of things now, without even any money of my own to keep things afloat."

"You could sue him," she said.

"Sandy, we've had this conversation before. Everything Ben and I had together was based on handshake deals. He was my friend, so I trusted him. Now I have nothing to stand on in court."

"That's ridiculous, David! How can the law just let someone get away with stealing from you and ruining you?"

David was speaking in a monotone at this point. "Sandy, I know it sounds unjust–it is unjust–but he didn't do anything illegal. And it hurts, because I trusted him . . . but from his point of view, he trusted me as well. And for most of the last year or so I've been neglecting my side of the business, obsessing over how much money I could make in crypto. So yeah, I trusted him, and he trusted me–just like you trusted me. Looks like all three of us made bad bets."

The confused mélange of spousal love and violent rage she felt was becoming too much, and Sandy began to shut down emotionally. Her voice went flat. "So what else is left?"

"A few thousand in the joint checking account—about enough for a month's living expenses."

"My God, David, how can this have happened? You were a self-made millionaire. How could you possibly go broke?"

David laughed bitterly. "Two ways: suddenly, then all at once."

Sandy grimaced with irritation at his paraphrase of an Ernest Hemingway line and gave him the mother of all withering looks. David was joking, as he always did when he was under stress. But flippancy on his part was wildly inappropriate under the circumstances, and she was in no mood to let him get away with it. "I need to take a shower and clear my head," she said. "I can't even think."

And with that, she got up and walked out of the room.

CHAPTER 2

DELUSIONS AND EPIPHANIES

After running the water for a minute to get the temperature right, Sandy stepped gratefully into the shower—the place where she always did her best, most productive thinking. *And oh boy*, she thought, *do I have a lot to think about today.*

Was it really only a couple of hours ago that the contours of her life had been the same as what she'd always been accustomed to? Only yesterday she and the kids had been at the horseback riding class they'd been taking together—something they would not be able to afford anymore. Ditto the kids' soccer, their piano lessons . . . a long and rapidly growing list of the elements of everyday life now suddenly seemed to sit on a high shelf, unreachable.

As she worked shampoo into her hair, Sandy tried to imagine where her conversation with David would pick up when she finally left the temporary respite of her shower. She could ask him a thousand more questions about the details of what had happened, but really, those details were trivial. She knew the important fact: her family's security had been shattered, as had her trust in her husband. That she never in a million years would have imagined him capable of such impulsiveness and such dishonesty was more than disconcerting—it was profoundly disorienting. It was like awakening from a nap to find yourself on an alien planet and being told by that planet's indigenous little green men that you'd *always* lived there.

Having finished shampooing, Sandy began to rinse the suds from her hair, and found herself trying not to hyperventilate. She had to keep her head together. As bad as this gut-punch revelation was for her, how much worse would it be for Amy, Chelsea, and DJ?

Especially DJ. Tears sprang to her eyes as she pictured her boy, a sweet child who thought his father was Superman, Einstein, and Abraham Lincoln all rolled into one person, reacting to the news that his hero couldn't be trusted even to keep a roof over their heads.

Of course, she reflected, lots of kind and perfectly decent men were failures at life—but the problem was worse than that. While Sandy still couldn't see David as *indecent*, her faith in his decency had been badly shaken by the facts. He had *stolen* from her. Stolen money from his own wife. That he'd expected to be able to turn what he'd stolen into a gift for her didn't let him off the hook for that crime. Whatever delusions David had harbored about the safety of the bet he'd made on Ephemerum, on some level he had to have known that what he was doing was wrong—because he hadn't *asked* her for that money. He'd taken it secretly (somehow), because he knew she'd say no if he asked.

If she had caught David having a one-time fling with his pretty secretary, Deloris—maybe in a situation where they were working late together one night—she might have found it in herself to forgive him.

Anyone can succumb to a moment's temptation to do something wrong, she thought. *People are imperfect—we're only human, after all.*

But this wasn't an impulsive tryst. It was deliberate, sustained deception to cover up reckless behavior that, even in a best-case scenario, would still have presented a danger to the well-being of their entire family, because get-rich-quick schemes were inherently risky.

And the best-case scenario had not materialized.

Sandy's sudden change in perspective was now casting familiar aspects of her husband's personality and mannerisms in a different light. He'd always been bold and aggressive in business and had been fond of the adage that it's better to ask for forgiveness than for permission. A bitter sarcasm crept into her thoughts. *How's that forgiveness thing workin' out for ya, Davey?*

And that was a pretty good question, come to think of it. How exactly *was* forgiveness for this transgression going to play out? Of course she'd forgive him—she had to, didn't she? And yet, suddenly, she couldn't imagine how she was actually going to do that. She desperately *wanted* to forgive him; her marriage and her children were now all she had left in the world. And yet, she couldn't make forgiveness happen by a mere act of will. Right now, she was too angry at David to forgive him, and she had an intuition that even when her anger faded—if it ever did—she'd find that her heart had hardened toward him.

And that was that. Although in the coming weeks she would no doubt vacillate, working her way through endless cycles of rage, pity, and self-doubt, she understood in this moment that her marriage was effectively over.

Sandy turned the water off and stepped out of the shower. Even as she toweled herself dry, the vacillation started: *We'll talk to a lawyer,* she thought, nonsensically, *maybe everything isn't lost. What he did was bad, but it doesn't have to mean the end of a twenty-five-year marriage. We'll get counseling. We said, "for better or worse," and this is the "worse."*

Below the level of her conscious thoughts, however, she knew this was a fantasy. And consciously, even as she tried to entertain the thought that they'd ultimately make it through this period of tribulation, she also knew she needed to get away from him for a while.

Now, showered and dressed, hand on the bathroom doorknob, she hesitated. She was suddenly frightened of how it would feel to look at his face again. She loved that face, and she couldn't bear the thought that when she saw it again, she'd probably want to swing her fist into it as hard as she could.

~

Sitting on the living room couch, David heard the water shut off and looked at the clock. It was 11:30, and Sandy had been in her shower for a good thirty minutes. He tried to imagine what she might be thinking, but his mind was too discombobulated to focus. He waited, agonizing over the time that had passed and worrying about how she might be feeling.

After what seemed like a hundred years, he heard the bathroom doorknob turn, and then her footsteps approaching. He raised his head anxiously . . . but quickly lowered it again in shame and fear. His eyes remained locked on his shoes as he heard her enter the room.

"David," she said after a moment. "Look at me."

He lifted his head again and looked up at her. She was dressed more plainly than when she'd gone out earlier—just jeans and a T-shirt. No makeup. No nonsense. There was a palpable distance between them now, and the sudden unattainability of her affection somehow made her more beautiful to him.

"I don't want to see you for a few days," she said. "I need time to sort out my feelings. Can you please go to a hotel while I do that?"

David's mind, searching frantically for some shred of hope he could cling to, seized on the phrase "for a few days." A brief sense of false relief washed over him—she was angry, but she'd get over it soon, and then things would somehow go back to how they'd been before that morning.

But then a nasty piece of reality forced its way into his thoughts: he *couldn't* go to a hotel—he was too broke. He put his head in his hands and went back to staring at the floor. "I . . . I can't afford it, baby," he said.

Sandy sighed, needing no further explanation to appreciate his position. "Then call a friend," she said. "Or go to a homeless shelter. Do *something*, I don't care what. Get creative. Just be out of here before the kids get home from school today, *please*."

"Okay," he said. "Anything you want."

"I'm going out for a while," she continued, reaching for her purse. "Please be gone by the time I get back." And with that, she opened the door, stepped through it, and shut it behind her.

David listened ruefully to the sound of Sandy's footfalls on the front steps—not heels this time, but no-nonsense flats—and presently heard her car start and the sound of its tires rolling down the driveway.

Okay, he thought. *What do I do now?* Unlike Sandy, David had no family to turn to. His parents had waited until their forties to have children and had not lived to see David reach that age. His only sibling, his brother Hank, had succumbed to alcohol-induced cirrhosis of the liver ten years ago.

Could he call a friend? Whom could he call? He was forty-six years old. Most men his age had families, just like he did. Whom did he know well enough to impose on in that way? Like many men his age, David had seen even his best friendships grow somewhat distant in recent years, as the lives of his old high-school and college buddies grew more consumed by the demands of careers and families of their own. It wasn't that those friendships were gone—just that there was a little more distance now than when they'd been twenty-six. He still spoke to three or four of those guys, but only once every month or two.

Ha! Maybe I should hit up Ben, he thought. *Lord knows, he owes me.* Of course, David knew that his erstwhile partner, Benedict Howey, might have a different perspective on who owed what to whom. It was a pointless line of thinking, really, just a way to indulge in the sad luxury of self-pity—but it sparked an idea: Ben wouldn't have helped David even if he could, but *the office* he and Ben had shared was still there, even if the two of them were no longer there to work out of it. And because the rent on that space was paid up to the end of the month, David still had the keys. There was a couch to sleep on, a phone, a break room with a microwave and a fridge . . . and a sink that could be used for personal hygiene, in a pinch. It was less than ideal, to put it mildly, but it was cheaper than a hotel.

Having some plan of action momentarily invigorated David, enabling him to shed the weight of depression long enough to pack a few necessary belongings and get moving. As he put some clothes into a suitcase, he reflected on the chain of events and decisions that had led him to his ruin. The sudden loss of everything he'd ever bought, built, and earned gave his mind some clarity, deflating the grandiose self-image he'd unknowingly constructed over the past few years. Most embarrassing, in the sober light of this morning, was the sense of invulnerability in which he'd cloaked himself—the notion that his judgment was infallible, his intelligence so extraordinary that the casual, half-assed crypto research he'd done had made him an expert on the subject.

He'd been exceptionally lucky in life, he now realized—far luckier than he'd ever deserved. Lucky to have succeeded as he had; lucky to have won the affections of a woman like Sandy. Perhaps he'd even been lucky to have found a business partner like Ben—not a visionary like himself, but a grind who had the patience to put countless hours into the tedious, unglamorous work necessary to run a successful business.

He hadn't just been lucky—he'd been *too* lucky for his own good. His luck had blinded him to his own limitations. Born on third base, he'd imagined he'd hit a triple. Over time, this luck had made him almost pathologically overconfident, and that overconfidence had swelled into arrogance.

He had stuffed his suitcase with all the clothes he'd need for a week or so. As he walked into the bathroom to collect his toothbrush and razor, David reflected that he knew of only two remedies for his perennial boredom: traveling to new places and finding fresh ways to make easy money. The one trip they'd taken to Las Vegas had addressed both of those needs, but Sandy had put the brakes on him when it came to hitting the blackjack table. She'd always been the sensible, cautious one—for which he both loved and resented her.

Maybe that was why he'd gone behind her back to put their shared financial resources into Ephemerum . . . to *show* her how smart he was: "You see? Look how much money you have now—money you wouldn't have had if I'd let your cautiousness hold me back!" He wouldn't have actually said such an unkind thing, of course . . . but he wouldn't have had to. The facts would have spoken for themselves, proving him right.

But he *hadn't* been right. He'd ignored the voice of reason coming from his own mind, a voice that sounded a lot like Sandy's. He'd ignored numerous red flags, not because he couldn't see them, but because he hadn't wanted to believe what they told him. He'd known that cryptocurrencies were inherently volatile, and that Ephemerum in particular was prone to wild fluctuations in value. But he'd also known that over time, the value of Eph had tended to rise. It would lose half its value in one quarter, then quadruple the next.

That was just excuse-making, though. Its general upward trajectory notwithstanding, Eph was far too volatile to serve as a safe parking spot for all the material wealth David and Sandy had ever amassed. No cryptocurrency was that safe.

And the danger could come not just from the coins themselves, but from the exchanges on which they were traded. The 2019 implosion of Canada's largest crypto exchange, QuadrigaCX, provided ample lessons about that danger. Quadriga's CEO and sole director had died suddenly and unexpectedly of intestinal obstruction, peritonitis, and septic shock while traveling in India. Upon his death, nearly $200 million worth of various cryptocurrencies belonging to 115,000 customers was discovered to be missing. Some of that money was suspected to have been embezzled, but much of it had disappeared simply because it existed only in offline "cold wallets"—data storage devices for which only Quadriga's late CEO held the passwords. Hundreds of millions of dollars in wealth had been destroyed in an instant.

Finished with his packing, David ran through a quick mental checklist: clothes, toothbrush, razor, laptop, tablet, blood pressure pills—he had everything. He closed his suitcase, grabbed his car key, and stepped out the front door of his house. He threw the suitcase into the passenger seat of his Porsche 911, hopped into the driver's seat, started the engine, and backed out of his driveway, still ruminating.

Ephemerum, ultimately, had been destroyed not by the theft of coins, but by the sudden collapse of the public's faith in those coins. Now, in parallel, David had been destroyed by his own faith in Eph—and by his misplaced faith in himself. That faith was now shattered. Eph's multiple vulnerabilities were exactly the kind of thing that he, a cybersecurity expert, had been trained to spot. Indeed, his ability to do this was what had made him wealthy in the first place.

David had done much of what he did out of wanting to believe in his own talents. But as he now realized, wanting to believe something makes you susceptible to delusion. And David had been deluding himself for a very long time.

CHAPTER 3

SUFFER THE CHILDREN

Sandy sat in the driver's seat of her Volvo XC60, parked at the curb in front of Rodenberry Middle School, where DJ would emerge in about ten minutes. Her afternoon had passed in a hazy blur. After walking out on David (she didn't like the implications of that phrase, but walking out was quite literally what she'd done), she'd gone to a nearby diner to sit with a cup of coffee and figure out what to do next. She'd sat in a booth in the rear corner of the restaurant, pretending to read a book, for over three hours, during which time she'd drunk about five cups of coffee—which hadn't done her nerves any good at all.

Because her thoughts of David were so confusing and upsetting, she resolved to put them aside as best she could (for now, anyway), and concentrate on just putting one foot in front of the other: what did she need to do next? Obviously, the top priority of the moment was to ensure that Amy and Chelsea and DJ understood what was happening, and that they were okay—at least as okay as could be expected under the circumstances.

Unfortunately, having walked out of the house before noon, she'd found herself with several hours to kill before the kids got out of school. Amy and Chelsea's school day ended at 2:15, and the girls always took the school bus home. (At fourteen and fifteen years of age, respectively, they'd rather have died than be seen getting picked up by their mom.) They normally spent the remainder of the afternoon hanging out with their friends, but today Sandy had texted them both, asking them to be home by 3:30.

DJ, who got out of school at 3:00, likewise usually took the school bus home, but today Sandy wanted him home earlier than the bus would have gotten him there. She needed all three of her children to arrive home at around the same time, if possible. Otherwise, she didn't think she'd be able to bear the suspense of waiting for them, a secret cloud of doom hanging over her head while she tried to maintain a façade of everyday good humor.

Looking up, she saw that the school's front doors were now propped open, and a dozen or so children were already making their way into the freedom of a mid-May afternoon, with no more classes or social pressures to deal with until tomorrow morning. Within a couple more minutes, the crowd of schoolchildren in front of the building would quadruple in size, so she began scanning the group, hoping to spot DJ in case he failed to spot her car.

She needn't have worried. About half a minute later DJ appeared, his book bag slung casually over his right shoulder, the breeze ruffling his blond hair as he approached her car, smiling at the surprise of a quick and easy lift home.

"Hi, Mom!" he said as he opened the door and hopped into the passenger seat. "What are you doing here?"

Sandy had rehearsed her answer to this question, but her stomach fluttered nervously just the same. "I was in the neighborhood, running errands," she said, knowing that every eleven-year-old translates the phrase "running errands" as "boring grown-up stuff that doesn't merit a follow-up question."

In keeping with his trusting nature, DJ accepted this and asked no further questions. He didn't even think to ask why she wasn't at work.

Sandy appreciated the serendipity of David's bad news coming on this long-planned day off from her job. She was the office manager for a large dental practice and her responsibilities there made it difficult to take time off. She'd asked for a personal day several weeks ago, when she'd learned that Lorna, her best friend from college, was going to be in town on business. They'd met for breakfast that morning before Lorna's afternoon business meeting and had tentative plans to go out for dinner that night—plans that she'd had to cancel after her confrontation with David.

She resented David for ruining this day, which she'd been looking forward to since mid-April, but she was simultaneously grateful for the coincidence. If today had been more typical, that sad, ugly scene would have played out with all three children at home.

When Sandy and DJ walked in the door at 3:20, she felt yet another surge of gratitude; Amy and Chelsea were already home, and more important, David was gone. The girls had made themselves tuna sandwiches and were seated on the couch in the living room, watching TV and happily munching away.

"Hi, Mom," Chelsea said. "We got your text. What's so important, anyway?"

Sandy suddenly felt a sour, black hole in the pit of her stomach. She took a deep breath. "Now that we're all here I can tell you. Turn off the TV, okay? DJ, take a seat on the couch with us."

The children did as they were asked and stared expectantly at her . . . and Sandy began, slowly, to speak.

~

When she'd finished, she felt cheated, somehow. She'd expected to be filled with a sense of relief after unburdening herself, but no such feeling came. She also felt ashamed of the details she'd left out, however necessary the omissions had been. With the worst, most unpleasant facts missing from the story, what remained had amounted to "Your father and I need to spend some time apart. We still love each other, and of course we both love all of you very much, *yadda-yadda-yadda . . .*"

She couldn't yet bring herself to tell them that her marriage was probably over and that their family was about to disintegrate, although as the day had worn on she had become increasingly certain that this was the case.

All three children were silent. The girls' faces were expressionless; DJ's cheeks were streaked with tears, but he made no sound.

Then, suddenly, the silence broke—it was like the delayed *boom* you hear several seconds after the flash of a faraway fireworks explosion. DJ's breathing got louder and took on a distressed, asthmatic sound, and then he began to sob like the little boy he still was. The sound was too much for his sisters, and the stone faces they'd been wearing abruptly melted into grotesque Halloween masks of grief. Crying herself, Sandy tried, as best she could, to put her arms around all three kids at once. When had they gotten too big for her to do that easily?

~

David, the invincible star pitcher, stood on the mound in his USC Trojans uniform. Seated among the fans behind home plate were Sandy, Chelsea, and Amy—and right behind the plate squatted DJ, his face bare because he'd forgotten his catcher's mask. David yelled to his son, trying to remind him to put his mask on, but the distance was too far, and his words disappeared into the wind.

Ben Howey stood at the plate, expectantly waiting for the pitch, a bat made of cryptocurrency waggling above his right shoulder. David wound up and threw the ball . . . a wild pitch that refused to fly in the way he meant to throw it. Ben swung, but he never had a prayer of hitting that ball—his bat was made of Ephemerum, after all.

"Swing and a miss!" David heard the TV announcer's voice in his head as though he were at home watching the game. And even as the announcer called the play, the ball hit DJ squarely in the face. Blood went everywhere, and the boy exploded into tears. David stood helplessly on the mound, unable to reach his injured son . . .

. . . and awoke on his office couch with a panicked cry. He sat up, breathing heavily and sweating, as the nightmare receded.

He looked up at the clock on the wall. It was 2:47 a.m.—too early to get up. He'd have to try to get back to sleep somehow. Below the clock stood the small liquor cabinet he kept for certain client meetings.

David wasn't generally much of a drinker, but right now the thought of a shot of Maker's Mark to calm his nerves was irresistible. With a plaintive sigh, he got up and went to the cabinet, and poured himself a drink.

Although tonight had been the worst yet, he'd had one variation or another on that dream every night since Sandy had thrown him out. The particulars varied, but two themes were consistent, night after night: injury to his wife or children caused by his own ineptitude—and baseball. He supposed that neither of those dream images were surprising. He was dreaming about hurting his family because . . . well, he'd hurt his family. And he was dreaming about baseball because it was the only thing he'd been good at before he'd gotten into the cybersecurity business. (Which, in light of recent events, seemed to mean that baseball was really the *only* thing he'd ever been good at, period.)

He'd gone to USC on a baseball scholarship, excelled as a pitcher there, and then pitched in the minors for four seasons before hitting a wall in AAA-level competition. As he approached thirty, it became clear that his childhood dream of pitching for the Dodgers was never going to come true. Fortunately, disappointing though that realization was, David's future as a bitter, working-class ex-jock wasn't written in stone. Besides being a talented (if not quite MLB-level) ballplayer, he also had a knack for technology. So, at the age of twenty-eight, he was hired by a SoCal bank to work in their cybersecurity department. He quit within a few years to start his own cybersecurity consulting business with his college buddy Ben Howey. They called the company SafeTech, and by the time he turned forty-five, David was worth twelve million dollars.

Tonight was his third night on his office couch, and thankfully, it would be his last. Sandy had called earlier that day to inform him that she was taking the kids to her parents' house with no timetable for return. In the morning, he would be able to return to his now-empty home.

Thinking about that empty house, the nightmare image of DJ's bloodied face still fresh in his mind, he downed the shot of Maker's, grimacing as it slid down his outraged throat—this was a big reason why he seldom drank. Nevertheless, he poured himself another while he waited for the bourbon's calming effect. The second shot was bigger than the first, but he decided to sip the whiskey this time rather than shoot it.

As they did every night, his thoughts soon turned to, *How the hell did I get here?* He looked around the office, taking in all its familiar shapes: his desk, with his iMac sitting in the center of it; the liquor cabinet; the bookcase; the whiteboard; the expensive chairs in front of the desk, where clients used to sit. David suddenly found himself overcome with an unexpected wave of nostalgia. He'd spent a lot of good years in this room, and he'd made a lot of good money here. Surely there must be some way to return to that life?

Of course there wasn't. Ben had seen to that. And to be honest . . . David had seen to it that Ben had few other options, and no motivation to be anything but ruthless about their parting of ways. For the past year and a half, while David had grown ever more obsessed with his cryptocurrency research and acquisition, Ben had taken on an ever-increasing share of the workload.

Their practice was incredibly successful, and they both deserved credit for that success. Gregarious by nature, David was a natural when it came to dealing with clients and putting them at ease. He could talk with charming self-deprecation about his experiences pitching to college batters who had gone on to become some of baseball's biggest stars. He managed to impress them with how close he had gotten to playing in "The Show," and yet he never sounded like a braggart or a blowhard. He was just a good guy to talk to, or to play a round of golf with.

He'd also made great choices in terms of hiring his team, so everything seemed to be essentially on cruise control—which ultimately caused him to become bored. And that was his undoing. He began to neglect day-to-day operations, leaving such details to his trusted number two, Ben. David would show up for critical client meetings, but otherwise he spent long hours locked away in his office, watching the crypto market . . . while Ben seethed with resentment.

David didn't care about Ben's resentments, though, and ignored his occasional complaints. They'd both gotten rich from this company, hadn't they? Meanwhile, David was getting even richer from his crypto investments—even as his once-flawless personal touch with clients began to deteriorate slightly. Without realizing it, he was starting to become a bit of a bore on the subject of crypto, the kind of person one avoids at cocktail parties, and with whom one dreads having a business meeting.

As David sipped his second pour of whiskey, the first began to take effect—his anxiety lessened, but even as the alcohol took the sharpest edge off his pain, he grew more melancholy, brooding over the ugly end of his relationship with Ben.

He'd gotten so self-absorbed that he failed to give any thought to developments in their business relationship that should have been disquieting. For one thing, despite being overworked, Ben was beginning to take an interest in the client side of the business—*David's* side of the business. He was taking meetings with clients . . . sometimes without David present. "I've got the Jeff Anestis situation under control," he'd say, "so don't worry about it. Go play golf with Tom Trapotsis today. You get along with him better than I do."

In hindsight it was obvious: Ben was sidelining him, and he didn't even realize it.

And then one Friday it all came to a head. At the end of the day, Ben came into his office and said something one usually hears from a girlfriend who is about to leave: "David, we need to talk."

Uh-oh, David thought. *No pleasant conversation ever follows those words*. And sure enough, what followed was very unpleasant indeed.

"David, I've been trying to talk to you about this for months now, but you haven't listened. You haven't been pulling your weight, and because of that I'm drowning in work. It's not fair, and I can't take it anymore. I'm dissolving our partnership."

David flashed his best thousand-watt, major-leaguer-postgame-interview smile. "Ben, come on. You're not being fair. Besides, what will you do without me? How will you bring in business? Do you even have a vision for what your future would look like as a solo operator?"

A half-smile appeared on Ben's face for an instant, and then was gone. "I think I'll do just fine," he said dryly. He pushed his glasses up his nose. "You may be surprised."

"Surprised?" David's thousand-watt smile vanished, and his voice grew thick with sarcasm. "Ben, if there's one thing you've never done in your entire life, it's surprise me. You don't have my knack for client relations, and you don't have my business vision. All you have is a gift for the grind. If we have problems, then let's talk about them and see whether we can work them out. But don't for one moment think that you don't need me."

Expressionless, Ben maintained eye contact for several seconds, and David abruptly saw the futility in talking any further. "Fine," he said. "Go, then. Get the hell out of my office."

That enigmatic half-smile appeared again for an instant, and Ben stood up and walked out, leaving David to contemplate the mystery of it.

By mid-morning the following Monday, however, that little *Mona Lisa* face of Ben's was no longer a mystery: he'd taken two-thirds of their clientele with him. Just as damaging, he'd taken most of the staff, leaving David with nothing more than the office itself—a desk, a computer, a few chairs, and a couch he'd eventually end up sleeping on.

Looking back on that day, David grimaced with embarrassment. It hadn't even occurred to him that Ben *could* do such a thing, much less that he actually would. Still, as infuriating as that Monday morning had been, he'd taken it in stride at the time. *To hell with him,* he'd thought. *I made more from Ephemerum alone last quarter than I made the entire previous year with SafeTech. And that's not even counting my investments in Bitcoin, Dogecoin, and others. I don't* need *this business.*

And that was that. Over the next few weeks, David went about fulfilling his remaining business obligations, during which time he also let his clients know he was closing up shop. He dismissed his remaining staff with generous severance payments and informed his landlord that he'd only need the office for another month.

Then he went home, took another look at the ever-escalating value of Ephemerum, and made the fateful decision to go all in on it . . . *all* in.

And now here he was, broke and ruined. He eyed the bottle of Maker's Mark. Deciding against a third shot, he flopped back down on the couch and tried going back to sleep.

As David pulled his Porsche into his driveway the next morning, he found himself tearing up a little at the sheer familiarity of the place. *Hello, David*, the house seemed to say. *Welcome home.*

Of course that feeling dissipated the moment he stepped through the front door. The emptiness of the place was overwhelming, and he realized he'd never actually seen the house like this. For as long as he'd lived in this house, *someone* had always been here whenever he came home to it—someone who loved him. He sighed. *Maybe I should get a dog*, he thought. But he knew that was out of the question given his allergies. Besides, the kids had each begged for a dog from the time they could talk; how would it look to them if he got one for himself after refusing them for so long? He was going to have a tough enough time holding on to their affections as it was.

He'd spoken to the kids only once in the four days since Sandy had walked out. It hadn't gone all that well. He'd told them a simplified version of the truth: Daddy had made some big mistakes with the family's money, and Mommy was mad because he'd done it without including her and now they were going to have to look for a smaller house. Although gratitude was pretty low on the list of emotions he could feel strongly anymore, he did feel grateful to Sandy, in a distant, abstract way, for not telling them the really bad stuff. She'd left it to him to decide how much to fess up to.

DJ had cried, mostly, and pleaded with him to come home. Amy had done likewise, although, being older, she'd done a better job hiding and controlling her tears. Chelsea, however, had been accusatory. She knew that something was being kept from her, and it made her furious. "What did you *do*, Daddy?" was practically the only thing she'd said, and her voice when she said it had sounded so much like Sandy's that David could hardly bear it.

He looked around the house. At least most of the furniture was still there—Sandy had taken her favorite chair and the credenza she loved, but everything else was still in place. Still, what she had taken was enough to upset him afresh: the absence of her chair, all by itself, was evidence that she intended to be gone for a good long time. The missing credenza had even more ominous implications.

DJ's Little League trophies were missing from their place of honor atop the cabinet in the dining room, and the kids' rooms were starkly empty of all but dressers and beds. He shut his eyes as they filled with tears. This wasn't how you packed up your kids to spend the summer at Grandma's. This was how you packed for a permanent move. The Shallcross family, with the exception of David himself, was *gone*.

And if he didn't think of some way to set himself straight, and soon, he was going to follow them . . . and not to his in-laws' house. Not for the first time, his head spun at the realization that a week ago he'd been a multi-millionaire. Now he was thinking he should look in the garage for a box that would be big enough to sleep in but small enough to drag to a choice spot under the 101 freeway.

Walking past DJ's room on his way back to the kitchen, he glanced inside and noticed something he'd missed before. The room wasn't completely empty. One item remained in the far corner:

the boy's piggy bank. His first thought was that the disintegration of DJ's family—he was now the product of a broken home—had pushed the kid into some kind of early adulthood. (He was eleven, after all—a little old to be saving his allowance in a ceramic pig.) But sticking out from underneath the pig was a note.

His curiosity aroused, David walked over to the bank, picked it up, and opened the note:

Dad,

I wish you and Mom could work out your problems and you could stay with us. PLEASE try. But if you can't, it's OK. Mom says there's money problems and we might lose the house. I hope not but if you need money here's some to tide you over.

Love,

David Shallcross, Jr.

David noted that the boy had signed his full name—not "DJ," but "David Shallcross, Jr." He smiled a little as he got the subtext—the kid was affirming his connection to his father, and his devotion to him.

Inside the pig was a whopping forty-eight dollars. David was so touched and so overcome with grief that he thought he might be sick. Obviously, he couldn't accept this money; the next time he saw the kids he'd have to find some way to return it gracefully and gratefully. What had he done to deserve such a sweet child?

Nothing, replied the other side of his mind. *You don't deserve him or Amy or Chelsea, and you never have. That's why you've lost them.*

Accepting all these thoughts as truths, David sat down on the floor of DJ's room (now DJ's *old* room) and began, not for the first time this week, to cry. His utter ruination was finally impressing itself on his mind. This wasn't some ordinary financial crisis that he could ride out by stiffening his upper lip, tightening his belt, and putting his nose back to the grindstone. Nor were he and Sandy having an ordinary fight that could be worked out in the bedroom, or even in a marriage counselor's office.

No, this was a crisis of an entirely different order. In fact, it wasn't even really a "crisis" at all. A crisis is something that can be addressed, dealt with, or managed. This situation would allow him to do none of those things. Through his own stupidity and recklessness, he'd destroyed twelve million dollars—twenty years' labor, gone in an instant, *while he slept.* And just as stupidly, he'd betrayed his wife's trust, which she might one day forgive, but could never forget in the way that wives and husbands need to be able to do. His children still respected him (or at least DJ and Amy did), but that would last only until they grew old enough to know better—as Chelsea apparently already had.

I've destroyed myself in every way but one, he thought. *So why not finish the job?*

David wasn't a big gun nut, but he owned a Glock-19 that he kept for home defense. He hadn't touched the gun since the last time he'd been to the firing range, about five years ago. He kept it in a gun safe in the bedroom closet.

Gritting his teeth, he went to the bedroom and fetched the weapon. He then returned to the living room and sat cross-legged on the floor in front of the couch.

He took a deep breath, exhaled slowly, and carefully put the barrel of the gun in his mouth.

CHAPTER 4

"CLICK."

Sandy looked around her old room—correction: it was now *her room*, period—with a sense of *déjà vu* similar to what David had experienced upon returning to their marital home a few hours before. It was like some strange kind of time travel. *Hello, Sandy*, the room seemed to say. *Welcome home.*

After stewing in her grief and anger for a few days, she had come to a few rational conclusions about what to do and how to move forward. Given the sudden, radical change in their circumstances, it didn't make sense to stay in the house where she and David had lived since before Amy was born. They would have to sell the house sooner or later, so why not move out sooner? At least her parents' home was in the same school district, so the move would not be overly disruptive for the kids. Or, rather, they would at least be spared the additional disruption of changing schools.

Besides, the aggregated memories were too painful. David's absence was overwhelming, both for her and for the kids. His electric razor no longer sat on the bathroom sink, nor did his towel hang on the wall next to it. The fridge no longer contained the microbrew he liked and always kept on hand. His Porsche was missing from the driveway and his clothes from the closet. His shoes no longer sat by the front door. In nearly every corner of the house, it seemed, some everyday sign of David to which they were all accustomed was gone, leaving a conspicuous vacuum in its place.

All this was reason enough to move, but Sandy had an additional reason: it would make things at least a little bit easier on David. Although the bond between them was shattered, possibly beyond repair, she still loved him, and she hated the thought that he was suffering as much as she was (and maybe more, in some ways). He knew how badly he'd screwed up, and she pitied him for that knowledge.

Of course the house would hold just as many painful memories for him as it did for her and the kids, but at least it was a home—*his* home—and that would have to make it a friendlier, less depressing place than his office couch every night.

So, after a terse phone conversation in which she informed David of her decision, she'd taken the kids and moved in with her parents. She hated the necessity of this move. She knew her father had been enjoying his retirement, and she knew from her own experience as a wife and mother that no matter how much you loved your kids, it was nice not having them around sometimes. She knew that her parents' marriage had undergone something of a renaissance after she'd moved out following her graduation from college; she and her mother had even talked about it once. "Of course we loved having you here," her mother had said, "but after you left, I have to admit, there was an upside to you being gone. A sense of intimacy came back into our marriage."

Seeing Sandy's uncomfortable expression, she hastily added, "I'm not talking about the bedroom. I mean just sitting cozily together on the couch, watching TV, just me and him—nobody else home, or anywhere within earshot. I missed that while I was raising my kids, and I'm happy to have it back."

Sandy knew her father felt the same way, and she hated to have to impose on them both now. And yet . . . there was no sign from them that they felt imposed upon at all. On the contrary, while they shared her grief (they'd always been fond of David), they also projected, subliminally, an air of barely restrained giddiness. Despite the sad circumstances, they were clearly delighted to have their grandchildren in the house and to have their daughter with them.

Whatever the reason, Sandy was grateful. She didn't know how long they were going to be living there—she couldn't yet think that far ahead—and she couldn't imagine what was going to become of David, but with her parents' support, she knew that she and the kids would come through this okay. She still had a career of her own. And although it might be tough for the kids to adjust to growing up middle class, rather than rich, the experience would probably build character in them.

"Sandy! Kids! Dinner's on!" Her mother's voice came suddenly and loudly from downstairs, snapping her out of her reverie, and her feelings of gratitude intensified. She had eaten little in the past few days, but now that it had been brought to her attention, she could smell her mother's beef Wellington, and she was pleasantly surprised to discover that she had an appetite—a big one, in fact.

Shaking and crying, jaw clenched, David released the trigger.

Click.

Click? That wasn't the sound David had expected to hear. Not at all. Really, he hadn't expected to hear *anything*. What he'd expected was that a round from the Glock would obliterate his cerebral cortex before it could register any sound at all.

Frustrated and relieved (although he couldn't admit the latter emotion to himself), David slowly, cautiously withdrew the weapon from his mouth. After staring at it in befuddlement for a minute, he examined the gun.

The magazine was empty.

David blushed with embarrassment. He'd evidently forgotten a lot about guns in the five years since he'd last taken the Glock out of that safe. *Of course it's empty, you idiot,* he thought. *You've always been a careful, responsible guy—or at least you used to be—and a careful, responsible gun owner doesn't leave a loaded gun lying around a house where three curious children live.*

It would have taken him less than a minute to remedy the situation and try again, but the spell was now broken, and David was left confused. He lay on the floor in despair, mind racing, wondering whether he really wanted to do this. Only a minute or two after an awkward, undignified, failed first attempt, he suddenly couldn't imagine himself blowing his brains out. He's the only one who would ever know, of course . . . but he *would* know, and suddenly he just couldn't bring himself to exit this life feeling like such a failure that he couldn't even get this right. The drama of the moment was gone, and he didn't want to go out in such a ridiculous manner.

His head felt slightly clearer, and the ramifications of this impulse decision began to occur to him. He wouldn't have left a pretty corpse if he'd done it; the mess would have been ghastly. And who would have found his body? Quite possibly Sandy . . . or, God forbid, one of the kids.

Besides that, there were practical considerations to weigh. For one, they were going to have to sell the house soon—or, if he killed himself, Sandy would have to sell it, and she would have a much harder time doing that if he offed himself in the living room. People don't want to buy houses where other people have killed themselves, and word would get around.

David knew that beneath all the layers that make up the human psyche, nearly every human being has a basic, biological will to live. For this reason, many failed suicide attempts actually motivate the would-be self-destroyer to re-engage with the world. After a moment of reflection, however, David realized he was not one of those people. His humiliating failure had caused him to rethink the time and place of his demise, but it had not abated his desire for it.

Since he couldn't kill himself in the comfort and privacy of his home, where *could* he go? Now that he'd thought of it (and he was ashamed not to have thought of it before), it was suddenly very important to him that Sandy not be the one to find his body.

Not knowing where he was planning to go, and hardly aware of what he was doing, David went back to the bedroom closet, where his gun safe was bolted into the wall, and grabbed a box of ammunition. He then grabbed his car key from the kitchen table and walked out of the house, locking the door behind him. *Ha. Don't know why I bothered locking up*, he thought. *By this time tomorrow, it won't be possible for anyone to steal anything from me.*

Of course, that was a half-truth, he reflected. When he was gone, everything in that house that was his would become the property of his wife and part of his children's inheritance (what was left of it, anyway). Locking up was therefore the least he could do.

He got into his Porsche, stuck the gun and the ammo in the glove compartment, and started to drive. Looking down at the fuel gauge, he saw that the tank was almost full. *Where am I going?* he wondered.

He soon found himself cruising down Route 74, the Ortega Highway. That would take him past Lake Elsinore to the 15, which would eventually take him to the high desert. This, he soon realized, was where his subconscious mind was taking him. With that understanding, he decided that wherever he ran out of gas was the place to do the deed. After taking a moment to calculate where he was likely to end up, given his gas mileage and the size of the Porsche's tank, he concluded that he was probably headed for the northern Mojave Desert—to Death Valley.

"Well," he said aloud. "That's apropos . . . if a little too on-the-nose." He chuckled and turned on the radio, half-expecting to hear the Doors' grim epic, "The End." But the radio was playing Pharrell Williams instead: "Because I'm happyyyyyy! Clap along if you feel like happiness is the truth—"

David shut the radio off and drove on in silence.

~

By midafternoon, David had passed Barstow and entered the desert. In less than an hour, he reached Baker, a metropolis teeming with . . . 735 sunbaked souls, according to the most recent census. For a moment, he contemplated stopping for a bite to eat, and maybe to admire Baker's dubious claim to fame, "the World's Tallest Thermometer." Built in 1991, this pitiable attempt at a tourist attraction was exactly what its name promised: a 134-foot thermometer, whose precise dimensions served to commemorate the record-setting 134-degree temperature that had been recorded in Death Valley in July of 1913.

The temptation to stop was only momentary, however. David wasn't interested in giant thermometers, and he wouldn't need food where he was going. Resolutely, he turned left onto CA-127 and proceeded farther into the Mojave, toward his appointment in Death Valley.

About an hour later, he checked his fuel gauge and noticed that he was now well below a quarter-tank. He continued driving until the needle rested just above E, and then pulled off the highway and headed down a desolate dirt road that cut through a nearly featureless landscape, decorated only with sagebrush and the occasional saguaro cactus. It was May—not quite summer yet—so the temperature was only around 85 degrees, as opposed to the 110 degrees or hotter he'd have encountered had he made the trip in July or August. He drove for about half an hour on that road, passing no one—no other cars, no farms, no houses, no stores. High desert, pure and simple.

Finally, the engine sputtered and choked. He was out of gas. As the car rolled to a stop, he steered it to the side of the road and parked. He sat there for a minute, marveling that the most important hour of his life had finally come. He'd expected that he might feel butterflies in his stomach when this moment came, but his guts were cool and solid, his sense of purpose firm.

The ambient temperature was only eighty degrees, but the sun out here was relentless and unfiltered, and without the air conditioner running, the car's interior heated up quickly. It had been less than two minutes since he'd pulled over, but he was already becoming uncomfortably warm. *No sense putting it off*, he thought, and he reached into the glove compartment to retrieve the Glock and the box of ammo. By the time he'd finished loading the weapon, the air in the car was hot enough to drive him out.

David opened the car door and stepped out into the high desert. A light puff of a breeze struck his grateful face, which was already slightly flushed from sitting in the hot car for three minutes. But then the breeze was gone, and he soon began to wonder whether he'd imagined it.

He sighed deeply, sensing the arrival of a pivotal moment—one of his *final* moments. He closed his eyes and fixed the faces of his wife and children in his mind's eye; he wanted Sandy, Chelsea, Amy, and David Jr. to be the focus of his final thoughts. After meditating on their images for a moment, he raised his face toward the sky—eyes still closed—placed the barrel of the Glock under his chin and pulled the trigger.

Click.

For a moment, David simply failed to comprehend what had just happened—or failed to happen—to him. His bizarre first thought was that heaven was nothing like he'd expected . . . that it actually looked an awful lot like the Mojave Desert.

After about ten seconds, his rational mind reasserted itself. "You have *got* to be for-crying-out-loud *kidding* me!" he shouted into the empty wasteland.

He checked the safety—it was not engaged. Wondering if he'd lost his mind, he pulled out the magazine and looked into it: Yep. The gun was loaded. Of course it was—he'd just loaded it a couple minutes ago. Setting the magazine down on the hood of the Porsche, he pulled the slide back. There was no round in the chamber. Grunting with irritation, he replaced the magazine and pulled the slide back again; *That should do it,* he thought. He took aim at a nearby cactus and pulled the trigger, only to be rewarded with that same dry clicking sound again.

A voice spoke within his mind. *It's been probably five years since you've gone to the firing range, pal. When was the last time you cleaned or oiled this gun? When was the last time you performed* any *kind of maintenance on it at all?*

Suddenly furious, David wound his arm back like the star pitcher he'd once been and threw the useless Glock as far as he could. Then, groaning aloud in exasperated defeat, he leaned back against the car and slid downward until he was sitting on the ground with his back against the driver's-side door. Stuck out here in the high desert, the author of multiple failed violent schemes, he felt a bit like Wile E. Coyote. The thought made him laugh out loud for the first time in almost a week. *Okay, you "super-genius,"* he mused to himself, *now what?*

He couldn't go home. Not now. Not after all he'd done, not after trying so hard to do the right thing. He felt worthless. He felt like human garbage.

David stood up and looked off into the distance, wondering what to do. Then, without realizing that his body had already decided on his course of action, he began to walk.

CHAPTER 5

WALKING THROUGH THE VALLEY (OF THE SHADOW) OF DEATH

Before long, David had walked so far that he couldn't see his car anymore. It didn't matter. Where he was going, he wouldn't need a Porsche. He had left the road far behind—and with it, his path back to the world.

He kept going until the sky began to darken. He was now very hungry, having opted not to bring any food or drink with him. He was also tired, so he stopped walking, lay down on the ground, put his hands behind his head, and stared up at the sky. He'd stopped wondering where he was going hours ago; he figured he'd eventually fall asleep, and then some wild animal would find him and kill him. Or maybe he'd be surprised by a band of drug dealers sneaking through the desert. It didn't matter. The outcome would be the same either way; all that mattered to him was that it be quick and painless.

That being eaten alive by animals or dying of exposure might not be as quick or painless as he wished did not occur to David. Despite the sense of mental clarity he felt, an objective observer would quickly have ascertained that between the heat, the lack of food and water, and the despair he had fallen into, David was not in his right mind. But of course there was no objective observer here (or at least, none that David could know about). There was only him and the vast expanse of Death Valley.

Gazing meditatively at the full moon, David felt at peace for the first time since that terrible morning when he'd awakened to find that his life's work and everything he'd cared about had been vaporized. His life insurance would restore to Sandy and the kids some semblance of the lifestyle to which they'd become accustomed. Now he was prepared to pay the price for his mistakes with his own life, if doing so meant that his family would not have to pay it.

Oddly, his newfound sense of peace was accompanied by a strange feeling of liberation—he felt unexpectedly *free*. He had done something that, deep down, from time to time, most people dream of doing (although most wouldn't have done it this way). He'd *gotten off the grid*. No one knew where he was, and it might be weeks before his body was found—if it ever was. He'd left his phone in his car, so there was no temptation to call for rescue, or to see whether the Dodgers had won last night's game. No more email to return. No more errands to run. No more meetings or tax returns or trips to the DMV. He was free of all that. He wasn't dead yet (even if he soon would be), and in a weird way, he was more alive than he ever had been.

Fatalistically content in his despair, David fell asleep.

When he woke, hours later, it was full dark, and he was cold. The dry, rapidly cooling evening air had evaporated the sweat he'd worked up walking God-only-knew-how-many miles, and that process had stolen a lot of precious body heat.

How long had he been asleep? Without his phone, he had no way of knowing; he hadn't habitually worn a wristwatch since 1998. (He owned a Rolex, but he wore it only on special occasions.)

He shivered, realizing he'd left his jacket in the car, too. Maybe that was just as well; maybe death by exposure would be preferable to getting eaten by whatever prowled this wilderness.

"So, you're finally thinking about what it would mean to die out here, eh?"

The voice came from mere inches away, just over David's left shoulder, and it startled him so badly he thought his heart might stop beating on the spot. "Gaaahh!" he shouted. "What the—"

Sitting right next to him, as casually as if he had been there all along, was his college pitching coach, Paul Martland, the first person other than his mother who had ever taken an interest in his well-being.

David stammered. "Wh . . . what . . . who . . . Coach Martland?"

"No, it's Henry Kissinger," Coach replied, in a tone that conveyed disappointment—but no surprise—at his star pitcher's sub-par deductive skills. "Yeah, it's me. Who else would bother to show up and talk sense to you at a time like this?"

Not wanting to embarrass himself further—it had been an embarrassing day already, and he sensed that Coach knew it—David pulled himself together and quickly regained his composure. "Sorry, Coach. You snuck up on me, is all."

"That's more like it," Coach said, approvingly. "How ya doing, Davey?"

No one else, other than his mother, had ever called David "Davey." Sandy had tried the nickname once, and he'd rebuked her so sharply—more than he'd intended—that she never again used it, even in jest. But he'd never minded his mom calling him Davey, and for some reason he'd never minded it from Coach Martland. It was a way of putting him in his place, maybe, but that was okay coming from one of the few authority figures—maybe the *only* authority figure, other than his mom—whom David Shallcross had ever respected enough to obey.

"Good, Coach." David replied. "Real good."

Coach said nothing.

"Well, okay, I've been better, I guess." He paused, trying one last time to make sense of this absurd situation. "Coach . . . what are you doing here?"

Unsmiling—David had never, ever seen him smile—Coach Martland replied, "Never mind me. What are *you* doing here, Davey?"

For a moment, David felt as though his heart had crawled downward and wrapped itself around his solar plexus—that weird sensation one feels when one is about to cry. But then, mindful of Coach's eyes upon him, he mastered his feelings and pulled himself together. "I'm doing the right thing."

"Making orphans out of your children is the right thing, is it? Do go on."

Looking a man like Coach Martland in the eye wasn't easy, but David, like the rest of his Trojan teammates, had been trained mercilessly to do so just the same. Meeting Coach's gaze had a way of keeping you honest, both with him and with yourself; the man's gray eyes seemed to look right through you. He had a commanding mentor's aura about him, a personality and appearance like a cross between Clint Eastwood and Mr. Miyagi (or maybe a less-gentle version of Obi-Wan Kenobi), with perhaps a little touch of Ronald Reagan or JFK.

"Well, no, not when you put it that way. But it's not up to me anymore. I screwed everything up, and I can't provide for them anymore. This is the only way I can make things right. It's the only way for me to atone for the dumb mistakes I've made . . . betraying Sandy's trust, risking their futures . . . it's all I have left. I'm a bad father and a worse husband, and they'll be better off with me gone. With me dead, they'll be able to collect on my life insurance. They'll never have to worry about money. They'll be *taken care of.*"

Coach remained stone-faced, and David wondered if the man had even understood him. It was impossible to tell. Neither David nor any of his teammates had ever known much of anything about their tight-lipped coach. He never talked about his personal life—if he even had one. He seemed to have few interests outside the chalk lines that separate fair territory from foul. He had never married, and as far as anyone knew, he didn't date. The unspoken consensus among David's teammates was that Coach wasn't married simply because he'd never been *interested* in marriage. He had incredible focus, and that was what had made him a successful coach.

"So this is how you're going to take care of them. You ever known any fatherless children who were well taken care of, Davey?"

David had no answer.

Coach continued. "And how's that insurance money going to take care of them? Is a couple million gonna set them all up for the rest of their lives?"

"No, of course not. But it's enough for Sandy to re-establish herself. Once the bills are paid and she's bought a smaller house that she can afford, she can invest what's left in the stock market and build something that will take care of her and all three kids."

"Just like *your* investments took care of *you*, right?"

Ouch. That one really stung. David was a smart guy, but talking to Coach always made him feel like an idiot.

"Sandy can make it work," David replied. "She's a smart lady. She'll make the right choices where I couldn't."

Coach sighed impatiently. It was a familiar sound. As a younger man, David had read contempt into that sound. But now he was older, a parent three times over—and he heard something different in it.

"Yeah, she's a smart lady," Coach conceded. "But I think you know that's not enough. She doesn't have financial expertise. She's good at running things—that office where she works was a nightmare without her while she took emergency family leave this week—but she doesn't have the financial *experience* you do. That experience is part of your value as a human being, Davey. It's a small part, but it's something you have that she doesn't. It's part of your Human Life Value—what I call your HLV—and it's something she'll need."

David stammered again, in confusion. "H . . . L . . .?"

Coach ignored him. "Now, don't get me wrong. Sandy's got plenty of HLV of her own, but you can't discount what *you* bring to the table. And you can't just bail out on your responsibilities to her and your kids. It's wrong, Davey. It's cowardly."

David respected his old coach like a father, but he was a grown man now, not a twenty-year-old college kid, and he became indignant at this affront to his pride. "Cowardly? Now hold on a minute, Coach. *Cowardly?* I was about to sacrifice my *life* for them. I even went through with it. I pulled the freaking trigger—*twice.*"

Coach snorted derisively, unimpressed.

David went on, caught up in the flow of his anger and indignation. "And until that last screw-up, I provided for them all pretty well, didn't I? I mean, look at the size of the roof I put over their heads."

"If you say so," Coach replied, in a tone that suggested he might lose interest in this conversation at any moment.

"I sure as hell do say so. And never mind the size of the house—our family was worth over *twelve million dollars.*" David was suddenly struck by the absurdity of defending his record as a provider—a role he'd been prepared, a few minutes ago, to kill himself for failing to fulfill—and his anger deflated under the weight of his shame. "Well, we *were*, anyway, until I destroyed all the wealth on that balance sheet. And that's why I have to man up now and accept the consequences of my actions." Yet again, he felt close to tears, but managed to hold them back.

Coach's face relaxed slightly, and some of the sternness went out of it. He put his arm around David's shoulders. "Never mind the 'consequences of your actions' right now," he said. "Tell me about that balance sheet you just mentioned."

"Well, it was a spreadsheet—a list of all our property, all our assets. Everything we own. I was looking at it the night before everything went bad. Our house is worth about $3 million, although I guess Sandy will have to sell it for less than it's worth just to liquidate it as quickly as possible. The Porsche is a good $200,000 asset. And then there's my savings account, which until the Ephemerum debacle had—"

"Stop. Stop it. Stop talking, kid," Coach chuckled (still not smiling), and the sound reminded David of his interactions with his own children, especially when they were younger. There was exasperation in it . . . but also a little warmth, and maybe even a little affection. "That balance sheet of yours is worthless."

"Well, yeah, it is now. Ever since I went and—"

"I said stop." The sternness was back in Coach's voice now, and David shut his trap immediately.

Coach continued, arms folded across his chest. "I mean *the sheet itself* is worthless, dummy. It's the wrong way to measure your worth. And *your* worth is what we're talking about here, not the paper value of David Shallcross's toys and trinkets and bank accounts.

"Look at it this way, kid. We all have a *property value* balance sheet, like the one you're talking about, which lists assets and liabilities. *Assets* like real estate—especially if it's paid off—stocks, your car, your bank account, et cetera . . . versus *liabilities*, like unpaid home loans, college debt, and so on.

"But there is also another kind of balance sheet—an *HLV* balance sheet. Human Life Value. And just like that money-counting spreadsheet on your computer, it adds up your assets and liabilities.

"So what is an HLV asset? Those kinds of assets would include things like knowledge, experiences, values—stuff like that. It's who you are as a person. Your children are an asset—and so is the experience you had raising them. It taught you something about the world, about how people grow, and about yourself. Then there's the drive you have that led you to start that business of yours—"

"The one I neglected and allowed my partner to take away from me," David interjected.

"You shut your mouth when I'm talking, boy," Coach said. "Now, where was I? Oh yeah, your assets. You had an independent streak and a vision for how you could make money without working for someone else. Those traits are *assets* you have, even if you've squandered them the last few years.

"Now, that HLV balance sheet also has a *liability* side—bad experiences, negative thoughts, limiting beliefs, and so on. Limiting beliefs are a big one. People get in the habit of saying things like, 'I can't do that,' and 'I'll never be good enough.'

"In your case, limiting beliefs aren't a problem. But you have other liabilities. You get bored easy—that's a liability. You've got a weakness for self-pity—that's a liability. You can sometimes lose your head, like you did over that 'Eph-coin,' and that's a *big* liability. Anyway, you get the idea. All this week you've been freaking out that you wrecked all your assets—which you think are the only assets you have, but you're wrong—and you're afraid you're not going to leave anything behind for your kids. You're all wound up about your legacy. But you're missing the point, and you're thinking about the wrong kind of legacy."

David opened his mouth to interject . . . and then shut it again. Now was a time for listening, and besides, he felt that Coach would slap him, hard, if he said another word.

"What is a legacy, Davey? It's what we leave behind when we take the final dirt nap, right? And what kind of legacy were you hoping to leave for your children?"

David hesitated until he realized that this question wasn't completely rhetorical—Coach really expected an answer. "Well, I was going to leave them all that stuff on that balance sheet you said was worthless. The house, the car, enough money for them to do anything in the world they want to do. College educations paid for on my dime. You know . . . what does *any* parent want to leave to their kids?"

"Okay, that's fine, I guess," Coach said. "But what if you could choose to leave them only one of two things? Either the money and the stuff . . . or your own talent for making it. Which would you choose? Which of those gifts would be the better legacy for a parent to leave behind for his children?"

David grinned mischievously. "Can't I leave both?"

"Kid, if you're not going to take this conversation seriously, then you can just walk off into the desert and get eaten by a mountain lion for all I care."

"Sorry, sorry. Please go on."

"As I was saying, if we have to choose to leave behind either the cash we created or *how* we created it, then that 'how'—the lessons we've learned and accumulated as we go through life—is the more valuable legacy by far.

"*People* are assets; *things* are not. Therefore, HLV is the source and creator of all the property value in our lives. So if we want to make and keep more money, we have to first increase our HLV. Don't lock up your assets in an IRA—put 'em back into yourself first. Self-improvement is another way to boost the value of your HLV balance sheet.

"All my life, I tried to improve myself for my own benefit, but also in order to leave a legacy: for all of you guys on the baseball team. For the school itself. For everyone I came into contact with—the guy who fixes my car, the waitress who serves my coffee. So you always need to be working on being a better human being, and not just for yourself.

Do this out of self-interest, knowing that it will create abundance for you—and also for everyone you come into contact with. It creates a ripple effect, and those people will benefit from your example."

David wasn't easily struck speechless—and he wasn't now. "This jazz is all very interesting, but . . . why do you keep referring to yourself in the past tense like that? Saying stuff like 'I *tried* to improve myself,' for 'everyone I *came* into contact with?'"

Coach looked at David as though David had asked him how to tie the laces on his loafers. "Davey, come on now. I was sixty-three when I was your coach—when you were in college. You're nearly fifty now. How do you think I came to be right here just in time to talk you out of abandoning your wife, your kids, and your own self? You think a ninety-year-old man hikes across Death Valley all by himself and just happens to run into one of his old students right when he's in the middle of killing himself in the dumbest way he can think of? Small world, ain't it?"

Coach always had a talent for making you feel dumb, David thought. "Uh, right," he said. "So . . . so you're . . . I mean . . . how did you get here then? How did—"

"Kid, I ain't here to answer trivia questions. I'm here to straighten you out—like I straightened out your curveball."

David was thunderstruck; here was something he'd never heard before. "Coach, did you just make a *joke?*"

"Jeez, if I'm gonna take questions like that, we could be here all night. Let's not sit here. I feel like walking. You feel like walking? A little while ago you were all set to walk until you dropped dead in the desert. C'mon, walk with me." Coach turned and headed into the darkness of the Mojave.

As it happened, David didn't feel a bit like walking. He needed to think over what he'd been told, and he wanted to sit while he thought. "Actually, I'd kinda like to sit and think for—"

The howl of some kind of wild animal cut him off. It didn't sound especially close . . . but it didn't sound as far away as he would have liked, either. Not wanting to be left alone with whatever had made that sound—wherever it was—David sprinted to catch up to his mentor.

CHAPTER 6

THE BIRD IN YOUR HAND

Coach wasn't running, only walking, and yet David found himself struggling to keep up. It was disconcerting—not to mention frustrating—because David had a lot of questions, and he didn't know how he was going to get his head together to ask those questions if Coach wouldn't stop to let him catch his breath and think for a moment.

"Coach, wait. Hold up a minute. I still don't get this 'HLV' stuff. I mean, sure, I have some good personal qualities—I can charm people, I have big-picture business vision, and I can throw an eighty-eight-mile-an-hour fastball. But so what? When you have as many negatives happening in your life as I do now—when you're as deep in the red as I am, HLV-wise—then what good can all that do me?"

"You're still leaving some important stuff off that HLV balance sheet, Davey," Coach replied.

"Like what?"

"*Relationship capital* is also a line item on your HLV balance sheet. And all your life, you've been blessed with huge amounts of relationship capital—which you've mostly squandered. Remember, people are assets; things are not. A home, for example, has no value whatsoever until a human being *gives* it value. Your wife was an asset of incredible value. Heck, who knows—maybe she still could be. Same goes for your children. And your friends, too, if you have any left. When's the last time you went to a ball game with your buddies?"

David didn't answer—he couldn't remember. *To be honest*, he thought, *it's been so long since I've seen Rick or Daryl, that it would feel weird to call them. Like asking your Uber driver for a date.*

After a brief pause, Coach kept talking, as though the question had been merely rhetorical. "It's been a long time since you've socialized with anyone who wasn't a colleague or a client. At some point, you lost interest in hanging out with anyone unless there was something you wanted from them. You were already sitting on a big pile of money and property—your property balance sheet—but you got obsessed with making that pile larger. You started to calibrate your sense of self-worth by bogus metrics like your bank account, your house, your car, your Rolex, et cetera. Why did you do that?"

Why did you do that? It was yet another question. David realized that this had always been Coach's teaching style: asking you questions, rather than telling you things you already knew, and thereby forcing you to come up with the answers on your own.

"I guess it was because before that, my self-esteem was wrapped up in my fastball. You remember what I was like in college, right, Coach? How good I was?" He affected the voice of Marlon Brando in *On the Waterfront*: "'I coulda been a contender, Coach, instead of a bum.'"

Coach grunted with disgust. "Good thing you didn't hang your self-esteem on your talent as a comedian. But yeah, you were a decent starting pitcher, although I've seen better."

"Aw, come on. Who was ever better than me?"

"Kid, I never thought your little jokes were funny, and I swear I'll leave you for the mountain lions if you make me remind you of that one more time. Anyway, as I hope you know, no matter how good you are, there's *always* somebody better. And no matter how good you were, even if you'd had a career in the majors, it'd all be over with by now, wouldn't it? You're what, forty-four?"

"Forty-six," David replied, sullenly. He suspected Coach knew exactly how old he was and had feigned ignorance just to make him say it aloud himself. It was a mean trick, but it drove the point home.

Still, as bitter a pill as it was to swallow, Coach was right. Baseball *hadn't* been a very good or durable hook to hang his self-esteem on. The chances that he was ever going to stand on the pitcher's mound at Dodger Stadium were always pretty small, and even if his dream had come true, it wouldn't have lasted. *Then* what would he have done about his perpetual boredom?

When everything had failed to work out according to his dream, he'd thrown himself into entrepreneurship as a substitute for baseball. He tried to compensate for the endless ache inside him by demonstrating to the world—and himself—how valuable a person he was through his work. But deep down, he'd never believed it, so he'd compensated by spending money on tangible symbols of success—the house, the Porsche, the Rolex, and so on.

He realized that he had been looking at things backward, placing all this value on his financial balance sheet and ignoring his HLV. He understood now that he had never considered himself his number one asset. He hadn't properly valued the focus, presence of mind, hard work, and commitment it had taken for him to become a successful pitcher, a successful business owner, and a successful husband and father. At some point, he had given up on educating himself, figuring that he knew all he needed to know about everything. After all, didn't his big house and fancy car prove how much he knew about life?

Coach had been silent for a while, but now he spoke again. "Anyway, getting back to the subject of relationship capital . . . you've got a nasty habit of throwing that stuff away, don't you?"

"What do you mean? I didn't throw Sandy away. She left me."

"Oh, well that's different then, isn't it?" Coach's sarcasm was like a shrink ray from some bad old sci-fi film, and David suddenly felt about an inch tall. "You had *nothing* to do with it, her leaving you. It just *happened*."

"Yeah, I get it, Coach. No need to rub salt in the wound. I know it was my fa—"

Coach cut him off. "Never mind. I do have a personal responsibility lecture for you, but I'll save it for later. I wasn't talking about Sandy, anyway. I was talking about Ben Howey—another instance of you throwing away relationship capital."

David was incredulous. "Ben? That snake? What kind of relationship capital was that? He stabbed me in the back and stole my livelihood. I'm well rid of him."

"Are you? And just how did you end up *getting* rid of him? How did you come to a place where he was doing a thing like that to you? Was it all just an accident of fate? Was he just a bad person from the get-go? If he was, then why did you go into business with him in the first place?"

Ugh, you're right again, you vicious old drill sergeant. "Okay, fine. I guess we had a few good years together. And I guess I couldn't have made SafeTech what it was without Ben. And I guess I got a little carried away with that crypto business. And maybe I wasn't pulling my weight those last few months. So I guess he had good reason to feel resentful. And maybe he felt like he had to do what he did in order to protect his own livelihood."

"And so?"

David sighed in defeat. "And so I guess Ben was another piece of good, valuable relationship capital that I threw away, like you said."

Coach chuckled mercilessly. "Good boy. It sounds like you're finally starting to listen to me. Hey, wow, would you look at the time."

David was about to say he didn't have his watch, but then he noticed that he could see his surroundings a bit more clearly than before. It felt as though he and Coach had only been walking together for about a half hour, but the sky was getting lighter.

"Wait, how can it be almost dawn already?" he said.

"Time gets funny out in the high desert," Coach replied. "Besides, there was a pretty long spell when you were thinkin' and we weren't talkin'. You must have lost track of the time."

David realized he'd spent half a day and all night wandering around in the desert. He supposed he should be hungry, but he wasn't. "How the heck could I lose track of fourteen hours?"

"I dunno," Coach replied, his tone indifferent. "Maybe you were impatient for the time to pass, so you zoned out. That would actually be pretty much in character for you, anyway. One of the many liabilities on your HLV balance sheet is impatience. It's one of your core personality traits, and that's why you get bored so easily. Which is why you like to gamble."

"Gamble? I'm not a gambler. I've been to Las Vegas one time in my life, and the only gambling I did there was playing a few slot machines for a bit. I didn't even play very long."

"Only because you got bored with the slots," Coach said. "And besides, you knew Sandy wouldn't have liked it if you sat down at the blackjack table. But you *are* a gambler."

"What do you mean?"

"What was all that crypto-investing about, if not gambling? Sure, you did a little bit of research, but did you ever really think you were an *expert* on crypto? Is anyone an expert on that stuff? No, nobody's an expert, and that means that investing in cryptocurrencies is gambling. Any investment you don't understand is a big gamble. Heck, playing the stock market in any way at all is a form of gambling.

"And that's the trouble with our society," Coach continued. "Everything and everyone, everywhere around you, encourages gambling. All those big financial institutions on Wall Street put a lot of effort into selling you this false promise—that high risk equals high return. But they never mention what happens to that return when the risk doesn't pan out.

"The question, then, Davey, is *why* do you gamble? You do it because you get bored so easily, which makes you impatient. You were bored with your business because it was doing so well. You were bored with all the boring stuff you were invested in—stuff that was boring *because* it made you money safely and reliably. Do you know that old expression, 'A bird in the hand—'"

"Is worth two in the bush. Yeah, thanks for the refresher on old clichés, Coach."

"Never mind that it's a cliché, dummy, and don't interrupt me. The point is that you're never satisfied with the bird in your hand, are you? No matter how pretty it is, no matter how sweetly it sings, you're always going after the one you don't have, because you think you'll get some kind of satisfaction out of that. But do you ever?"

This was obviously another rhetorical question, so David said nothing. He glanced up at the sky. It seemed like only a couple of minutes ago that he'd noticed the sun coming up, but now it was high in the sky. Judging from its position, in fact, it had to be nearly noon.

Coach went on. "No, you don't. You never get the satisfaction you think you're going to get from constantly pursuing whatever you think you need that you don't have. And your disappointment keeps you on an endless treadmill, running and running, chasing something you'll never catch.

"Like every other human being, Davey, you've got four basic psychological needs. The first three of those needs are certainty, significance, and love. Sandy represents those things for you, and always has.

"And yet some part of you feels like that's not enough—and that's because of the fourth need: *un*certainty."

David's brow wrinkled in confusion. "Wait, that doesn't make sense. You just said people need *certainty*—so how can uncertainty also be a need?"

"People do need security," Coach replied, "but they also need novelty. Adventure. Variety. *Risk*, even. And there's nothing wrong with that. If people didn't have that need, then nothing would ever get invented or discovered. Nobody would ever travel.

"But the trouble begins when some people get carried away. Everything is always too safe for them, too boring—sound familiar? They change jobs a lot, and lose out on the chance to establish themselves. They go through a lot of girlfriends or boyfriends, always wanting to be with somebody new, and then one day they find themselves alone and unloved. They take unnecessary risks—again, does that sound familiar?"

"Yeah," David said, staring at his shoes. "I guess it does."

Coach continued. "Certainty, uncertainty, significance, and love are the four basic needs, and yet, a lot of people still aren't fulfilled even when they have those needs met. They may be fulfilled to a certain point, but they soon find themselves wanting more, and *seeking* more. And that's where most people get into trouble.

"It's important to be *conscious* of the risks you're taking, and then to be deliberate about *how and where* you're taking that uncertainty. Take it in an area where you have control and knowledge and expertise, where you have purpose and passion, where you have Human Life Value. Don't take it in an area where you relinquish control of your cash. That is gambling.

"The trouble with you, Davey, is you start looking to fulfill those needs, and you go searching for certainty and significance in all the wrong places."

"Like in my financial balance sheets and my net worth," David said.

"Exactly," Coach said. He actually sounded pleased. "Now, a wife represents certainty, and that's an underrated human need. It's also the thing you're undermining when you gamble. And never forget, that's what your cryptocurrency adventures were—gambling. A good investment is something the investor can control, something they have knowledge and expertise in. If you don't have that knowledge or expertise, then you are gambling.

"If you're getting bored in your business, and you find yourself starting to look for solutions outside of your core business expertise, that is a red flag. Heck, it's not just a flag. It's a big, flashing red light, telling you—if you'll listen—to go back and look at your business and find some way to get inspired. Find *something* that motivates you to create in the area where you have knowledge and expertise and purpose and passion."

David suddenly began to feel lightheaded. For a moment, his entire life snapped into clear focus, and all the aspects of his own personality that he'd never been able to see became sharply visible. Then his vision went dark for a moment, and he fell to the ground.

He came to quickly enough . . . or at least he thought he had, until he saw that the sun was now in a mid-afternoon position. He'd been out here roaming the desert now for a good twenty-four hours.

He sat up, and found Coach sitting next to him, talking as though their conversation had not been interrupted. "Like I said, Davey, people are assets, things are not. *You* are your own number one asset . . . so you should be your number one investment."

David rubbed his eyes, which were dry and stinging. He was still listening to Coach Martland, but most of his attention was focused on the epiphany that was now breaking down the doors of his mind. "*I'm* the problem," he said. "Me."

Coach nodded. "Go on," he said.

"All my life, whenever anything went wrong, I never saw myself as the problem, so I never saw myself as the solution. But I *am* the problem—which means that fixing the problem is within my power."

Coach nodded, and almost seemed to smile. "It's time to take ownership of your life, Davey. And you can start by straightening out your sense of self-worth. That's probably the top line on your HLV balance sheet. Your sense of self-worth has always been out of whack. On one hand, you have a tendency to be haughty, to think you already have all the answers you'll ever need. On the other hand, you've never quite grasped that you yourself are the most valuable asset you own. Are you getting it now?"

"Yeah," David said. "I was always focused on my property value—my 'PV,' I guess you'd call it—but to increase that PV, I should have been focusing on my HLV."

Coach stood up, and with the sun behind him, David couldn't see his face—but he could swear the man was smiling. "You're getting it, Davey, and I'm proud of you. Your HLV is the source and creator of all PV in your life. It's a simple formula. Want to increase your PV? Start with your HLV. There are no bad investments, really—just bad investors."

"And I've been a bad investor," David said. "I've made money, but I've just been lucky—maybe too lucky."

Coach nodded approvingly. "Yeah, you got that right. You were lucky. But as with any gambler, one day your luck will run out. The money you earn is too precious to gamble with, because your life is too precious to gamble with. And when people relinquish control of their cash, when they let it go someplace where they have no knowledge or expertise or experience, they are gambling."

"I was gambling with my life," David said, awestruck. "And I nearly lost it."

"But when you truly understand your HLV," Coach said, "your decisions cease to boil down to just betting on red at the roulette wheel. Sure, you'll make mistakes. That's inevitable. But you can't dwell on your liabilities. Extract the lesson, apply it, and move on. Turn the liability into an asset.

"And when it comes to the financial side of things, remember, if you're going to relinquish control of your cash, you have to keep it protected and liquid. If you don't do that, then you're gambling with it—and you might just as well throw it away.

"The ultimate lesson, Davey, is that you have to invest in things you can control. Things you have knowledge and experience in. Instead of the stock market, invest in your own business, which you yourself control and operate. And keep as much as possible in cash savings. That's how you build yourself security. Invest in purpose and passion. Invest in *yourself*."

David tried to reply, but he found that he could no longer speak. His voice had grown progressively hoarser during their conversation, and when he opened his mouth, all that came out was a harsh, dry cough that doubled him over. The coughing became so intense that his vision began to swim around him again, blackness punctuated by a field of stars that pulsated in time with his hacking and croaking.

A loud whirring filled his ears, drowning out all other sounds. He fell on his face and found that he was too weak to stand up; it was an effort just to turn himself over onto his back.

As he lay there, a shadow passed over his face. Was it Coach Martland standing over him? He tried to open his eyes, but his face was turned up to the sky, and the sun was too intense to permit him to search for the source of that shadow. In the brief look at the sky he got in that fraction of a second he'd been able to keep his eyes open, it seemed as though some giant bird of prey were swooping down on him. This bird, he now realized, was the source of that whirring sound.

He'd learned his lesson too late, he realized, with a pang of regret. Coach had finally awakened him to his Human Life Value—and now he was about to be devoured by some kind of giant desert raptor.

He heard voices in his head, saying things that made no sense: "Where'd he come from? How'd he get all the way out here? Okay, I got the shoulders, you got the feet—lift on the count of three."

After all the suffering I've endured, David thought, *am I going to leave this world hearing weird voices in my head, getting torn apart and eaten alive by a giant bird? It's not fair . . .*

And then he passed out.

CHAPTER 7

RESCUE AND RECONCILIATION

David lay in bed, grateful to be there. He was alive, and grateful for that, too.

The bed he was so grateful for was not his own; he was in a hospital in Barstow. Death Valley National Park rangers had found him while on a routine patrol, looking for drug smugglers; their helicopter was the "giant whirring bird of prey" he'd been so certain was about to tear him to pieces. He was unconscious when they found him, badly dehydrated and sunburned, near death, thirty miles from his car—which had been vandalized and destroyed. Probably just kids, the sheriff had said, or maybe meth-heads. Either way, David's Porsche had been wrecked by bored people with nothing better to do, looking for an outlet for their boundless destructive energy.

Sheepishly, David had asked the sheriff, a mild-mannered, middle-aged guy named Ken Clark, whether a second set of footprints had been found alongside his own tracks.

"Are you saying that someone else was with you?" Clark asked. "Because we saw no evidence of any such thing."

"Never mind," David said, embarrassed. "I must have imagined it. Like I imagined the helicopter was a bird of prey."

He felt transformed by his experience—whether it had been real or not. Everything he had was gone or was about to be taken from him: his money, his investments, and his car were gone, and his house would be gone soon enough. Even his life insurance policy might not have paid off, he now belatedly realized. If he'd gone missing—if his body had been devoured by scavengers and never found—his permanent status as a missing person would likely have prevented Sandy and the kids from collecting benefits. Worse, it would have denied them closure, leaving them forever wondering what had become of him, and how he'd spent his final moments.

Whatever else he'd lost, he *did* still have his family, he now realized. Even if Sandy never came back, she would always be the mother of his children. The children themselves would always be his, and they'd always love him no matter how badly he screwed up. And if he still had their love, then he could win back their respect—even Chelsea's.

Moreover, he no longer felt that recovering from his self-inflicted financial apocalypse was a lost cause. He'd started one successful business from scratch, and he knew now that he could do it again. SafeTech had floundered because he had ceased to be a part of it in any meaningful way. Maybe the simpler, everyday aspects of running a cybersecurity firm didn't come as easily to him as they did to guys like Ben Howey, but that was largely a matter of discipline and focus. As long as he respected the HLV and effort that had gotten him there before, he could do it again.

He could probably even make himself rich again. Of course, that shouldn't be the point, he knew. But he also knew he could do it. And there was nothing wrong with thinking about making money. Yes, he knew there was more to life than numbers, but the numbers were important, too, as long as they were kept in their proper place. As long as he put his own Human Life Value first. *Dollars follow value,* he thought, *and money is a receipt.*

He realized now that his old way of living amounted to little more than gambling, and gambling wasn't the answer. He realized he needed to operate in a world of control, knowledge, and expertise. What he needed was a way to find certainty for himself, and for his wife and family—if only Sandy would take him back.

~

On his third day in the hospital, Sandy came to visit him. "Hey there, Tiger," she said, her voice cheerful, as though he were there to have a broken toe tended to. "I hear you got lost on your way to the tanning salon."

David laughed appreciatively. He had indeed gotten a fair dose of the sun's rays; his face and the back of his neck were still bright red and painful—as was the incipient bald spot he'd never noticed on the crown of his skull. *A near-death experience in the desert is a heck of a way to find out you're starting to go bald,* he thought.

"Everything okay at your folks' place?" he asked. "How are the kids?"

"They're getting by okay. My mom seems to have decided that their fridge isn't big enough to store all their ice cream, so she's trying to turn DJ into an ice cream storage unit. I'm worried that if we stay there much longer, he'll develop diabetes!"

David smiled. "I'm sure he doesn't mind." He paused, thinking about how she'd phrased that remark, and wondering whether he should comment or let it slide. He decided to go ahead and ask the question. "What do you mean, 'If we stay there much longer'? Are you thinking of going somewhere else?"

"You mean am I coming home?" she replied. David bit his lip and said nothing. She reached down to stroke his hair affectionately. "Maybe," she said. "Or maybe I'm just thinking about thinking about it. I miss you, and so do the kids. And we're all going to have to find a new place to live soon anyway, so maybe 'coming home' isn't the right way to think about it. But am I thinking about coming back to you? I really don't know."

She sat down in the chair next to the bed and took his left hand in both of hers. Of course he was still wearing his wedding ring, she noticed. And so was she.

They sat together like that for a minute, silently. Finally she said, "I wish there were some way for me to be sure that you'd never do anything like that again, David. You went behind my back. You *stole* from me. I never thought you were capable of doing something like that, and now . . . I just don't know what to think about anything, I guess."

"Well," David replied, "I sure have paid for my mistakes."

Her voice turned angry. "It's not about punishing you, David. I'm not sitting here thinking, 'Ha. Serves him right. He got what was coming to him!'"

"Yeah, yeah, I know that," he replied. "That's not what I meant. I mean that this experience was an extreme shock to my system. There's no way a man can lose everything that means anything to him, in the blink of an eye, and not be changed by it. This was a transformative event, Sandy." He paused to think for a moment. "Two transformative events, actually. First, I lost everything I had—and then I almost died. And in both cases, the negative events happened because I failed to appreciate what I already had in my hand. I lost everything because I thought that by putting it all at risk, I could gain more. And then I almost lost my life because I thought that was all I had to lose."

David paused again, trying to collect his thoughts. Sandy opened her mouth to speak, but he hushed her. "But I hadn't lost everything—not absolutely everything, anyway. I had a lot of time to think out there in Death Valley, and with everything stripped from me, even my car—the last thing I still owned, my only way back to the world—I got some new perspective. I still have my children, even if I never get to live with them again. And you're still the mother of my children, even if I lose you as my wife. That bond still means something, and it's not such an easy thing to destroy." Sandy squeezed his hand.

"Finally," he said, "I still have *me*. I still have my own silly life, and that life has *value*. I have talents that no one else has—just like everybody does. I managed to make something of myself once, and I can do it again.

"I wasn't always half-blind with greed, either," David continued. "But I did always have this restless streak in my personality. I just didn't see it for what it was. I thought it was moxie. Just ambition—a virtue. But it was more than ambition or drive. It was something destructive. And now that I know that part of me is there, and now that I see it for what it is, I can keep an eye on it"—he squeezed her hand—"if I have someone I can trust to help me do that."

Sandy smiled as tears came to her eyes. "You sound like a man who's learned his lesson," she said, and once again they sat together in silence for a minute.

Finally, she spoke again. "This is going to take an act of faith on my part, David. A big one."

"I know," he said.

"I mean, I really believe you. I really believe that after everything that's happened, you could never do that to me again. But . . . I believed that *before*. And I was wrong."

Again, David said nothing. David the salesman, David the charmer, the idea man who always had so much to say, was now silent in his newfound humility.

"But I guess I have to make that leap," she said. "Because I can't be without you. DJ needs you. Amy needs you. Chelsea needs you—especially because she thinks she doesn't. And *I* need you."

And she bent down and kissed his sunburned face.

~

They would start over, somehow, even if just on her salary to begin with. David had lost his money—*their* money—but now he had something better. He had a clear sense of who he was, and who he wasn't. He was now fully awake to his own intrinsic human value, and to the value of his family and everything else he'd risked and destroyed.

It wouldn't happen today, and it wouldn't happen tomorrow, but it was going to happen soon: David would rebuild his business.

He would apologize to Ben, to his kids, to himself. What mattered most, for now, was that he had his confidence again, and his sense of certainty that he was on the right track.

No more investments in crypto, or in anything else he didn't fully understand. Not because he had nothing to invest (he didn't, of course, although he soon would), but because he had learned the difference between investing and gambling, and he was done being a gambler.

The Porsche had been insured, and once his claim on it was paid, he could replace it with something more sensible (for now anyway). Like maybe a Toyota Tacoma . . . a used one. They would sell the house and move into a much smaller one, maybe even a rental. With the money they made from the sale of the house, and possibly a loan from Sandy, David would start fresh. The events of the past few months had damaged his reputation, but they hadn't destroyed it completely. If he patiently put his nose to the proverbial grindstone (as Ben had always done), he could rebuild his good name.

His children's faith in him was compromised, but perhaps that, too, could be spun into something positive. If Sandy could forgive him, then following her example, the kids could, too, and this event could prove to be a valuable growth experience for them. All three of them, even DJ, could now see that their father was a fallible human being, not a marble statue of a Roman god. And that understanding might enlarge their ability to empathize with others—because at some point in the course of their lives, they were all surely going to need to forgive, and to be forgiven.

Sandy sat with David until visiting hours were over, then left to return to her hotel room. David would be released from the hospital within a day or two, and then, like swallows, they would return to San Juan Capistrano. Sandy and the kids would stay with her parents for a while longer, while David remained in their house and started the process of selling it. Meanwhile, Sandy would look for a new, smaller home they could all move into together.

It wouldn't be the kind of life they were all accustomed to, but it would be enough. More important, David would never again put what he had at risk. He was finished with gambling. He was ready to live life the right way.

And that's exactly what he did.

AFTERWORD

The story you've just read is fictional, but it is not *entirely* fictitious. I have had my own gun-in-the-mouth moment, and that moment caused me to reevaluate my life and my worldview.

In 2007, like David Shallcross, I lost nearly everything I had. At the time, in the wake of that loss, I thought I was worth more dead than alive. Shaking, screaming, and crying, I stuck a gun in my mouth with the expectation that my life insurance policy would pay out, and my family would thereby be taken care of—economically, that is.

David Shallcross is not me, but there are many important similarities between us. Like me, David stopped believing in himself. He stopped growing. David didn't have an emphasis on his Human Life Value balance sheet. He had lost all his money in a bad investment, and the guilt and shame he felt destroyed his sense of self-worth. He didn't love himself—so then how could he love others? He lost his courage and his confidence—and like David, I lost my courage and my confidence. I felt like a piece of garbage. And because I didn't feel as if I had any worth, I didn't feel that I had anything to offer my wife or my kids or anybody else.

If you only looked at my financial balance sheet, you, too, might have said, "Yeah, he *is* worth more dead than alive." But that is a myopic view of life. When we evaluate what someone is worth, we are too quick to ask, "How much money does he have?" And that is why I wanted a new way to calculate the value of human life—so that people would see that they are worth much more than they might think.

My emergence from that dark period was the catalyst that motivated me to finish developing the concept of Human Life Value—which had already been in the works for several years. Between 2004 and 2006, my friends Garrett Gunderson, Ray Hooper, Les McGuire, and I came up with the Human Life Value Balance Sheet. Ray and Les died in a plane crash on June 8, 2006, but Garrett and I are still here, and I believe more than ever that the ideas we explored together are worth discussing and sharing.

The foundational premise of my work with Garrett, Ray, and Les is that people are assets, things are not; and Human Life Value is the source and creator of all property value. To be honest, I had forgotten all about it until I sat down with Garrett in 2011, and he said to me, "You can choose to leverage your past experiences to create forward movement, to extract the lessons from those experiences and apply them in your life, and then to share them with other people." It was Garrett Gunderson who put me on my path back into the financial services industry. Garrett believed in me, and he started sending me leads. That went a long way toward restoring my own faith in myself.

And then I went to work. And the more work I did on myself—building my courage and confidence back up so that I was able to take care of the four basic needs of certainty, uncertainty, significance, and love in my own life—the more I wanted to *continue* to grow and to share that with other people. So I did that, and I continue to do that today. Like my fictional doppelgänger, David, I am sometimes susceptible to boredom—and so I continue to challenge myself. I live a challenge-based lifestyle, which I learned at Wake Up Warrior from my dear friend Garrett White, who has assisted me greatly with this growth over the years and continues to do so.

While I'm acknowledging my debts, this is as good a time as any to note that I borrowed the concept of the "four basic needs" Coach tells David about from Tony Robbins at an *Unleash the Power Within* seminar. (Robbins actually postulates *six* human needs, the other two being the higher spiritual needs, growth, and contribution. [1])

When the four basic needs are met in our life, we seek more, in order to continue to grow and contribute to other people's lives. The best way I have found to grow and contribute is to challenge myself. This is what is meant by living a challenge-based lifestyle. Goals that stretch us. Challenge us. Targets that get us out of bed each day, excited to create. Asking ourselves questions like, "What would it take? Who would I have to become in order to [fill in the blank]?"

This is what I have done to earn back the money that I lost, and you can, too.

Step 1: Get clear on where you are.

Step 2: Ask yourself what you want in every area of your life.

Step 3: Get clear on why you want it.

Step 4: List the steps you must take in order to accomplish your goal.

---

1. Tony Robbins, "Discover the 6 Human Needs," https://www.tonyrobbins.com/mind-meaning/do-you-need-to-feel-significant/

When we challenge ourselves, we feel alive. It's fulfilling to be challenged, to create and exchange with others. Think back over your life up until today. What has brought you the most happiness and joy? Remember that success leaves clues. Identify those clues. Learn from others. Commit to lifelong learning.

This all fulfills us the most and creates the most for those around us. Then it's out of self-interest that we think and act this way. Not selfishness, but self-interest.

Appreciation and Gratitude

Here's another tool that has made a huge difference in my life and in the lives of countless people. I want to credit two major influences in my life, Garrett Gunderson and Dan Sullivan, CEO of the Strategic Coach program, for the idea. It sounds so simple that you may not believe it could make a big difference in anyone's life. But it does.

The idea is to keep a Gratitude Journal—to write down the things I appreciate, the things I want to celebrate, the things for which I want to express gratitude. It's a practice that I began not when I was on top of the world, but after I lost all that money and went through the experiences that got me where I am today. Journaling every day helps me focus on my own Human Life Value assets and motivates me to respect and appreciate them even more.

Most of us, me included, take too many things for granted in our lives—things that nine-tenths of humanity would be thrilled to enjoy: clean water. A clean place to live and a comfortable bed in which to sleep. Loved ones. An endless variety of delicious food to eat, places to go, and experiences to enjoy. We take all that for granted . . . and then we look at what other people have and wonder why we don't have *that.*

When I was rebuilding my life, I was reminded of something a recovering alcoholic once said: "I used to lie in the gutter judging other people's shoes." I may not have had much, but I wasn't grateful for what little I had.

Once I started my Gratitude Journal, though, everything changed. I started to notice what I did have instead of fretting over what I didn't have or what I'd lost. I had a positive focus to start my day, and my attitude toward life changed. This simple practice allowed me to feel more, and also to create more for those around me.

Sometimes we do things out of self-interest, and we mistake that for selfishness. But it's not selfish to express gratitude. There's nothing at all selfish about stopping to celebrate and appreciate the little and big things we get to enjoy every day. There's nothing wrong with giving ourselves that pat on the back; it actually creates momentum for us. It's not a pride or an ego thing. Instead, for me, it's an acknowledgment of the positive direction of my life, because until I started writing down what I was grateful for, I wasn't acknowledging my Human Life Value assets. I wasn't acknowledging the positive things in my life.

Gratitude Builds Momentum

The more I'm grateful for, the more I realize I have . . . and the more things I get to be grateful for. It's a gaining game. The more fulfilled we feel, the more we can create for others. To this day, I still write in my Gratitude Journal, in longhand, about what I celebrate and appreciate.

These days, I'm thankful for my health, my fitness, my mindset, my connection with God, my family, my relationship with my wife, my kids, my business, and my mental and physical strength.

My suggestion to readers is to use pen and paper—not a computer program—and start writing out every day what you're grateful for. I would encourage you to use the specific words *celebrate* and *appreciate*. Whatever you pay attention to grows, so the things you're grateful for actually become more numerous and deeper and even more precious.

It's okay to write down some of the same things every day—when are we *not* grateful for the gifts of life, health, and physical and mental strength? Anything that would belong on your Human Life Value balance sheet belongs in your Gratitude Journal.

If you're on top of the world as you read these words, that's great—you'll have a very long list for your Gratitude Journal each day. And if you're starting over, recovering from a catastrophe as I was, I'll share one more expression with you: When you're happy within, you can be happy without.

And gratitude makes us happy within.

Think about Your Legacy

I often ask my clients the same question that Coach Martland posed to David: If you had to choose between your Human Life Value or your property value, which would you rather leave behind? And every client I work with (or would *want* to work with—more on that in a bit) would rather leave the Human Life Value assets, the life lessons, and all of that.

But at the same time, I want to emphasize that property value is not a bad thing. You can leave both things behind—PV *and* HLV. It does not have to be either/or. Imagine a legacy estate plan that allows you and your significant other to leave not only the property value assets but also the more important Human Life Value assets.

Although David and Coach said so several times each, I feel I should be explicit here that I don't want to set up a false choice between Human Life Value and financial value or property value. I am not teaching people to despise money; far from it. Money is incredibly important. It is not *everything*, but it is an *important* thing. If you were forced to choose—if you could only leave either your HLV or your property value to your heirs—then you would do better to leave them your Human Life Value. But don't think for a moment that you have to choose.

Money is a tool. Money is a medium of exchange. Exchange creates wealth. Property value is a result of value created in exchange with someone else. As long as there is a free exchange—no deception, no coercion—then property value is one of the cornerstones of human civilization. That's not a trivial thing, even if it pales in comparison to HLV.

By your fruit ye shall know them (Matt 7:20). How do we know if what we have created is of value to someone? They are willing to exchange with us. Money is the medium of exchange that we use. Money could then be looked at as a receipt that says, "I value the value you created more than this dollar bill, and therefore I am willing to exchange it with you." And in that exchange, you are saying that you value the dollar bill more than the value you created and are exchanging. It really is a beautiful thing. Exchange creates wealth, and dollars follow value. Seek to create value and exchange with others. Ask always and often, "What is of value to others? What do I have to offer to exchange with others?"

Coach's question is best understood as a way to make you, the reader, think about the concept of *legacy*. Leaving a worthwhile legacy is what motivates a married businessman with kids to wake up and grind and create on a daily basis. When we think about what kind of legacy we're going to leave to the world (even if we don't have kids), it gives us purpose. It is out of self-interest, not selfishness, that we think about legacy. It fulfills you, and it creates the most for those around you.

In order to secure your legacy, you need to *own your life*. And by that I don't only mean you need to face up to your mistakes and misdeeds (although, of course, you do). I also mean that you need to take responsibility for the changes you want to see happen in your life. I also mean that you need to give your full and thoughtful attention to all areas of your life. What we give attention to grows. Always remember that, as Coach said in our story, *you* are your number one asset. Because people are assets; things are not. People make mistakes with their money all the time, but when they own them, they are free. I made some mistakes. I owned them all. I extracted the lessons and applied them, and now I am free.

Owning your mistakes means something else, too: you have a duty to forgive others *their* mistakes—especially members of your family. Coming together as a family, with forgiveness, is key to a prosperous life. Forgiveness is also the key to creation. If you want to create, you must forgive yourself and forgive others. True forgiveness opens up creativity. True forgiveness allows you to enjoy what is.

What I Do

I feel the weight and the trembling of the world. And that's okay. It's okay because I know what to do to help the world.

Many of my clients, when they come to me, are lost in one way or another. I provide an assessment that allows them to see where they are "at," as the saying goes.

Afterword

Where are *you*? When someone is lost, asking them that question enables them to reframe the way they're looking at their life, which in turn allows them to see exactly where they are, financially, in certain key areas of their life.

If you come to me for help, I'm going to assist you in figuring out exactly where you are with your money; it is about macroeconomics versus micro. I'll help you understand how to create certainty and realize that you are your own greatest asset, giving you permission to invest in yourself. I'll show you where to create the economic value of certainty as you store your money in the best place, protecting your family and your life. I'll assist you in understanding everything that you have going on financially on a macroeconomic level, so you can properly coordinate and integrate all your money decisions in a holistic manner.

I look at the big picture and take the complexities of macroeconomics and make them personal, relatable and simple. My role is coordination and integration to give you the tools you need to make comprehensive, holistic decisions.

We'll talk about principle-based decisions: How do you know if what you are doing with your money is the most efficient thing you can do? And is it principle-based? I'll share with you a principle-based approach that allows you to lower your risk and create more cash, consistently.

Financial institutions have an agenda. They want our money, they want it on a regular basis, and they want to hold onto it for as long as possible . . . and when it comes time for us to go and get our money, they want to pay it back to us as slowly as possible. Every product and service they manufacture is in service to that agenda.

The banks teach us to do one thing with our money, and then they do the exact opposite. So why don't *we* start thinking like a bank, and acting like a bank?

Why am I doing this? Because I want people to take their lives back. I want people to control their lives instead of letting others control their lives for them. I want you to own your current reality. I want to teach you to take action and follow through.

I have countless examples of business owners whose lives have been changed, who have seen firsthand how Human Life Value improves their quality of life and the profitability of their businesses. These people, my clients, have gotten rid of the distraction of having money that they were "gambling with"—money that they had relinquished control over, or invested in areas where they didn't have knowledge and expertise. They have redirected their assets into what they can control—their own business and their own careers.

Having said all that, you should know that I'm very particular about the clients I take on. First, I prefer to work with people who share my basic values on some level. Most of the people I choose to work with have a certain profile: they're usually career people, business owners and entrepreneurs, who are already saving money, or who at least have a *desire*, a deep internal drive, to start saving money.

If what I have to offer sounds like what you need—and if you want to avoid the kinds of harrowing, potentially life-altering experiences that David Shallcross suffered—then go to my website, Vaultais.com, and take the assessment on the home page. Then schedule a meeting. This is an investment in yourself, if you are ready to take a leap into a better life, with more certainty, love, (add in your other needs).

It's your legacy, your life. Let's get started . . .

ABOUT THE AUTHOR

Michael G. Isom
Founder of Vault AIS™

Michael Isom has dedicated his life to creating empowering conversations around production and protection.

Michael built the financial firm Vault AIS to help entrepreneurs and business people understand and leverage the principles underlying today's powerful and rapidly changing economic forces.

Co-Author of *What Would The Rockefellers Do*, Michael speaks to audiences across the country, inspiring business owners and professionals on The AIS Triangle™.

The AIS Triangle is a unique system allowing business owners, individuals, couples, and families to pay less in tax, safeguard money, access that money along the way, and earn interest versus paying it. The system ensures that money survives from one generation to the other and simplifies personal finance.

Michael lives with his wife, Wendy, in St. George, Utah.